WORLD POLITICS - BIG BOOK
World Governments Series

• • • • • • • • • • • • • • • • • •

Written by Darcy B. Frisina, M.Ed.

GRADES 5 - 8
Reading Levels 3 - 4

Classroom Complete Press
P.O. Box 19729
San Diego, CA 92159
Tel: 1-800-663-3609 | Fax: 1-800-663-3608
Email: service@classroomcompletepress.com

www.classroomcompletepress.com

ISBN-13: 978-1-55319-412-5
ISBN-10: 155319-412-8

© 2007

Critical Thinking Skills

World Political Leaders

Skills For Critical Thinking		Reading Comprehension												Writing Tasks
		Bush	Reagan	Castro	Fox	Peron	Thatcher	Gorbachev	Mandela	Gandhi	Arafat	Zemin	Dalai Lama	
LEVEL 1 Knowledge	• List Details/Facts		✓					✓	✓			✓		
	• Recall Information	✓	✓		✓	✓	✓	✓	✓	✓	✓	✓		
	• Match Vocabulary to Definitions		✓	✓	✓	✓		✓	✓		✓	✓	✓	
	• Label Maps	✓		✓	✓		✓				✓	✓		
	• Recognize Validity (T/F)	✓						✓						
LEVEL 2 Comprehension	• Summarize		✓			✓	✓	✓		✓	✓			✓
	• State Main Idea		✓	✓								✓		
	• Describe		✓		✓	✓		✓			✓	✓		
	• Interpret			✓					✓					
	• Compare/Contrast													✓
LEVEL 3 Application	• Organize Facts	✓	✓	✓					✓					
	• Use Outside Research Tools		✓	✓		✓					✓			✓
	• Application to Own Life			✓	✓	✓				✓		✓		
	• Apply Vocabulary Words in Sentences	✓					✓			✓				
LEVEL 4 Analysis	• Draw Conclusions										✓			
	• Identify Supporting Evidence				✓	✓	✓			✓	✓			✓
	• Make Inferences			✓					✓			✓		
	• Identify Relationships											✓		
LEVEL 5 Synthesis	• Predict			✓							✓			
	• Imagine Self Interacting with Subject											✓		
	• Suppose	✓							✓	✓		✓		✓
	• Create a Plan										✓			
LEVEL 6 Evaluation	• State and Support an Opinion		✓		✓	✓		✓				✓		
	• Evaluate Decisions Made by Subject									✓	✓			✓

Based on Bloom's Taxonomy

World Politics – Big Book CC5777

Critical Thinking Skills

World Electoral Processes

Skills For Critical Thinking	History of the Voting System	Legitimacy of Democratic Government	Presidential System	Parliamentary System	Dictatorship Government	Suffrage	Systems and Reform	Writing Tasks
LEVEL 1 Knowledge								
• List Details/Facts			✓	✓	✓	✓	✓	
• Recall Information	✓	✓	✓	✓	✓	✓	✓	✓
• Match Vocabulary to Definitions	✓		✓		✓	✓		
• Recognize Validity (T/F)	✓					✓		
LEVEL 2 Comprehension								
• Summarize	✓	✓		✓				
• Describe	✓	✓		✓	✓		✓	
• Interpret			✓	✓	✓		✓	
• Compare/Contrast			✓	✓				✓
LEVEL 3 Application								
• Use Outside Research Tools		✓	✓	✓	✓	✓	✓	✓
• Application to Own Life	✓							
• Organize Facts	✓							
• Apply Vocabulary Words in Sentences			✓		✓		✓	
LEVEL 4 Analysis								
• Draw Conclusions					✓			
• Indentify Cause and Effect						✓	✓	
• Make Inferences					✓		✓	
LEVEL 5 Synthesis								
• Prediction		✓					✓	
• Imagine Self Interacting with Subject	✓	✓	✓					✓
• Create a Plan								✓
• Imagine Alternatives			✓		✓	✓		
LEVEL 6 Evaluation								
• State and Defend an Opinion	✓		✓	✓		✓	✓	✓
• Evaluate	✓				✓			✓

Based on Bloom's Taxonomy

Critical Thinking Skills

Capitalism vs. Communism

	Skills For Critical Thinking	The Rise of Capitalism	The Industrial Revolution	Capitalism since the Cold War	Freedom of the Market & Individuals	A Capitalistic Political Economy	A Communist Political Economy	A Globalization Economy	Communism in the 21st Century	Writing Tasks
LEVEL 1 Knowledge	• List Details/Facts	✓				✓	✓			
	• Recall Information	✓	✓	✓	✓	✓	✓	✓	✓	
	• Match Vocabulary to Definitions	✓	✓			✓	✓		✓	
	• Recognize Validity(T/F)		✓		✓			✓		
LEVEL 2 Comprehension	• Summarize	✓		✓	✓					
	• Describe	✓				✓	✓	✓		
	• Interpret					✓		✓		
	• Compare/Contrast		✓							✓
LEVEL 3 Application	• Use Outside Research Tools	✓	✓	✓		✓	✓		✓	✓
	• Application to Own Life	✓	✓		✓			✓		
	• Organize Facts			✓						
	• Apply Vocabulary Words in Sentences			✓	✓			✓		
LEVEL 4 Analysis	• Identify Cause and Effect	✓	✓	✓			✓	✓	✓	
	• Make Inferences		✓						✓	
	• Draw Conclusions									✓
LEVEL 5 Synthesis	• Prediction								✓	✓
	• Imagine Self Interacting with Subject		✓		✓			✓		✓
	• Create a Plan	✓			✓			✓		
LEVEL 6 Evaluation	• State and Defend an Opinion			✓			✓			
	• Evaluate				✓					
	• Explain									✓

Based on Bloom's Taxonomy

Contents

● ● ● ● ● ● ● ● ● ● ● ● ● ● ● ●

Contents

FREE!

✔ **18 BONUS** Activity Pages! **Additional worksheets for your students**

✔ **18 BONUS** Overhead Transparencies! **For use with your projection system**

• Go to our website: **www.classroomcompletepress.com/bonus**

• Enter item CC5761 or World Political Leaders

• Enter pass code CC5761D for Activity Pages. CC5761A for Overheads.

• Enter item CC5762 or World Electoral Processes

• Enter pass code CC5762D for Activity Pages. CC5762A for Overheads.

• Enter item CC5763 or Capitalism vs. Communism

• Enter pass code CC5763D for Activity Pages. CC5763A for Overheads.

Assessment Rubric

World Politics – Big Book

Student's Name: _____   Assignment: _____   Level: _____

	Level 1	Level 2	Level 3	Level 4
Comprehension of Capitalism and Communism	Demonstrates a limited understanding of the concepts. Requires teacher intervention.	Demonstrates a basic understanding of the concepts covered.	Demonstrates a good understanding of the concepts covered.	Demonstrates a thorough understanding of the concepts covered.
Response to the Text	Expresses responses to the text with limited effectiveness, inconsistently supported by proof from the text.	Expresses responses to the text with some effectiveness, supported by some proof from the text.	Expresses responses to the text with appropriate skills, supported with appropriate proof from the text.	Expresses thorough and complete responses to the text, supported by concise and effective proof from the text.
Analysis and Application of Key Concepts (i.e., evaluates a situation, relates and applies concepts to own context, conducts research, and collects relevant information)	Interprets and applies various concepts in the text with few, unrelated details and incorrect analysis.	Interprets and applies various concepts in the text with some detail, but with some incorrect analysis.	Interprets and applies various concepts in the text with appropriate detail and analysis.	Effectively interprets and applies various concepts in the text with concise, clear and effective detail and analysis.

STRENGTHS:

WEAKNESSES:

NEXT STEPS:

Teacher Guide

Our resource has been created for ease of use by both TEACHERS and STUDENTS alike.

Introduction

Our resource provides ready-to-use information and activities for remedial students in grades five to eight. Written to grade and using simplified language and vocabulary, social studies concepts are presented in a way that makes them more accessible to students and easier to understand. Comprised of reading passages, student activities and overhead transparencies, our resource can be used effectively for whole-class, small group and independent work.

How Is Our Resource Organized?

STUDENT HANDOUTS

Reading passages and **activities** (*in the form of reproducible worksheets*) make up the majority of our resource. The reading passages present important grade-appropriate information and concepts related to the topic. Included in each passage are one or more embedded questions that ensure students are actually reading and understanding the content.

- The BEFORE YOU READ activities prepare students for reading by setting a purpose for reading. They stimulate background knowledge and experience, and guide students to make connections between what they know and what they will learn. Important concepts and vocabulary from the chapters are also presented.

- The AFTER YOU READ activities check students' comprehension of the concepts presented in the reading passage and extend their learning. Students are asked to give thoughtful consideration of the reading passage through creative and evaluative short-answer questions, research, and extension activities.

The **Assessment Rubric** (*page 7*) is a useful tool for evaluating students' responses to many of the activities in our resource. The **Comprehension Quiz** (*pages 52, 95 & 138*) can be used for either a follow-up review or assessment at the completion of the unit.

PICTURE CUES

This resource contains three main types of pages, each with a different purpose and use. A **Picture Cue** at the top of each page shows, at a glance, what the page is for.

Teacher Guide
- Information and tools for the teacher

Student Handout
- Reproducible worksheets and activities

Easy Marking™ Answer Key
- Answers for student activities

EASY MARKING™ ANSWER KEY

Marking students' worksheets is fast and easy with this **Answer Key**. Answers are listed in columns – just line up the column with its corresponding worksheet, as shown, and see how every question matches up with its answer!

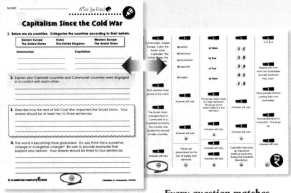

Every question matches up with its answer!

Bloom's Taxonomy

Our resource is an effective tool for any SOCIAL STUDIES PROGRAM.

Bloom's Taxonomy* for Reading Comprehension

The activities in our resource engage and build the full range of thinking skills that are essential for students' reading comprehension and understanding of important social studies concepts. Based on the six levels of thinking in Bloom's Taxonomy, and using language at a remedial level, information and questions are given that challenge students to not only recall what they have read, but move beyond this to understand the text and concepts through higher-order thinking. By using higher-order skills of application, analysis, synthesis and evaluation, students become active readers, drawing more meaning from the text, attaining a greater understanding of concepts, and applying and extending their learning in more sophisticated ways.

Our resource, therefore, is an effective tool for any Social Studies program. Whether it is used in whole or in part, or adapted to meet individual student needs, our resource provides teachers with essential information and questions to ask, inspiring students' interest, creativity, and promoting meaningful learning.

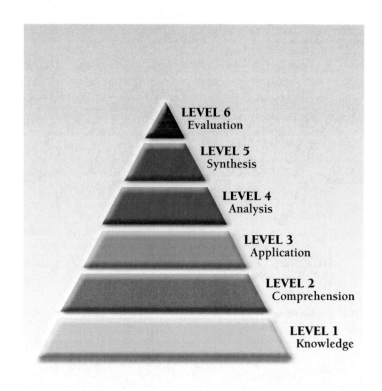

**BLOOM'S TAXONOMY:
6 LEVELS OF THINKING**

Bloom's Taxonomy is a widely used tool by educators for classifying learning objectives, and is based on the work of Benjamin Bloom.

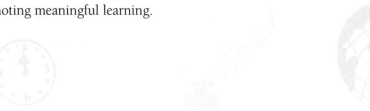

Vocabulary

World Political Leaders • World Electoral Processes
Capitalism vs. Communism
World Politics - Big Book

activist	corrupt	exposed	liberation	reduction
aid	corporations	figure	linked	reform
allies	coup	fled	manual	regulate
ambitious	course	fluctuating	medieval	reincarnated
ancient	decade	formidable	merchant	release
apartheid	demand	foundation	method	resistance
arms	democracy	fragmented	military	restore
assassinate	denied	fraud	monarch	rightfully
asylum	dictator	funding	monopoly	roles
bankrupt	disbanding	globalize	nations	shortage
beloved	dissolve	goods	negotiated	significant
bill	distant	gradual	notable	stabilize
cabinet	economy	groomed	obsolete	standard
cast	election	highjack	operate	stock
citizens	eligible	hostage	operations	strict
collapsed	eliminate	hostile	oppose	summit
colonization	embargo	indefinite	option	supply
commission	emerged	initially	organization	surplus
component	enforce	install	overthrow	term
compulsory	ensure	interact	parliament	terrorist
conflict	enterprise	intervention	permitted	threat
constantly	epidemic	isolated	persecution	transport
consumer	exception	immigration	personable	treason
controversial	execute	lax	published	waste
convicted	export	legislature	recognized	wealthy

NAME: _____

 Before You Read

George W. Bush

1. Complete each sentence with a word from the list. Use a dictionary to help you.

highjack	course	overthrow	disbanding
terrorist	conflict	controversial	

a) The party began _____ after the cake was served.

b) Paul and Ron are no longer friends because of a _____.

c) A _____ was caught before he could hurt anyone.

d) The people got together to _____ the unfair king.

e) We used a map to decide our _____ to the city.

f) The end of the game was _____ because the player may have been out of bounds.

g) Two people tried to _____ the car, but were stopped by the police.

2. The map has arrows pointing at three countries: the United States, Afghanistan, and Iraq. Using colored pencils, follow the directions below.

a) Color the United States **red.**   b) Color Afghanistan **blue.**   c) Color Iraq **green.**

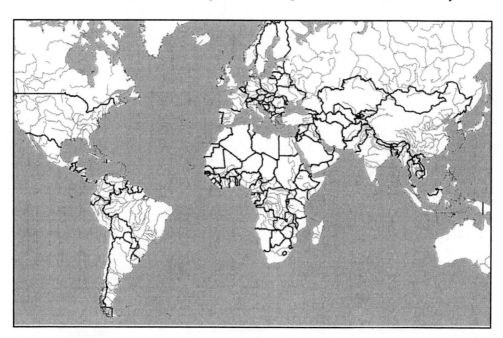

George W. Bush

George W. Bush was born on July 6, 1946. He is the 43rd President of the United States. His father, George Bush Sr., was the 41st President of the United States.

On September 11, 2001, Bush was visiting an elementary school when he learned that the Pentagon and the World Trade Center were attacked. Several people **highjacked** planes and flew them into the buildings. Thousands of people died that day.

This event set the **course** of his Presidency. Bush realized that the people of the world were not safe from **terrorists**. He decided to start a global war on terrorism. In 2001, Bush directed troops to invade Afghanistan, a country in central Asia. The purpose of this **conflict** was to **overthrow** the Taliban, a terrorist group.

STOP

Why did the United States invade Afghanistan?

_____

_____

_____

After **disbanding** the Taliban and helping the people of Afghanistan develop a democratic government, Bush focused on another country. In 2003, the U.S. military invaded Iraq. Bush wanted to help spread **democracy** in the Middle East. He also worried that terrorists would be able to get weapons from the Iraqi government and their leader, Saddam Hussein.

Bush's efforts in Iraq were **controversial**, but have had success. Saddam Hussein was captured and found guilty by an Iraqi court of crimes against his own people. Elections were held in 2005 to bring peace to the country and approve a constitution. Saddam Hussein was executed in Baghdad, Iraq by hanging on December 30, 2006.

NAME: _____

George W. Bush

1. (Circle) the word **TRUE** if the statement is TRUE **or** (Circle) the word **FALSE** if it is FALSE.

a) President Bush decided to send troops to Afghanistan to help the Taliban.
   TRUE   **FALSE**

b) President Bush was worried that terrorists could get guns in Iraq.
   TRUE   **FALSE**

c) Saddam Hussein helped spread democracy in the Middle East.
   TRUE   **FALSE**

d) Elections were held in Iraq to help approve a constitution.
   TRUE   **FALSE**

2. **Place the following *events* on the timeline below.**

Events: **a)** Elections were held in Iraq.   **d)** Troops were sent to Afghanistan.
         b) Saddam Hussein was found guilty.   **e)** Troops were sent to Iraq.
         c) The U.S. was attacked on
             September 11, 2001.

3. George Bush was also the **Governor of Texas**. In your own words, tell what you would do if you were governor of your state. How could you improve the state in which you live? Your answer should be two to three sentences.

_____

_____

_____

 Before You Read

NAME: _____

Ronald Reagan

1. **Read the definitions on the left. Find the correct definition on the right and write the correct letter on the line provided. You may use a dictionary to help you.**

a [ ] _____ A : Weapons

b [ ] _____ B :

c [ ] _____ C :

d [arms] _____ D :

e [beloved] _____ E :

f [ ] _____ F : Dear to the heart

2. **Before Ronald Reagan was president, he was an *actor*. Make a list of *at least five* ways his experience as an actor may have helped him when he was a president.**

a) _____

b) _____

c) _____

d) _____

e) _____

3. **Reagan told another world leader to tear down the *Berlin Wall*. Use the resources in your classroom (encyclopedias, books, the Internet) to learn more about the Berlin Wall. Find *three* facts to share with your class when you discuss the Berlin Wall as a group.**

a) _____

b) _____

c) _____

Ronald Reagan

Ronald Reagan was the 40th President of the United States. Before he was elected, Reagan had two very different jobs. He was a very famous movie actor in Hollywood. After he stopped acting, Reagan was also the Governor of California.

Reagan earned the nickname "The Great Communicator" because he was able to deliver speeches in a personal manner even in formal settings. He was also known to have a quick sense of humor and a positive attitude.

Reagan was also a **formidable** world leader. His presidency occurred during the Cold War, a time in history when the U.S. and Russia were struggling to get along. He began his **term** by starting an **arms race** with Russia. He knew that Russia would run out of money before the U.S. When this happened, Reagan signed a series of arms **reduction** treaties with Russia. This was an important first step that helped end the Cold War.

> **STOP**
>
> **How did the arms race help bring an end to the Cold War?**
>
> _____
>
> _____

The presidents before Reagan were unsuccessful in ending the Cold War because they tried to ignore the problem. Reagan confronted Russia head-on, even working with Russia to find common ground. Towards the end of his presidency, Reagan visited Mikhail Gorbachev, the leader of Russia. In a very famous speech, Reagan told Gorbachev to "...tear down this wall", referring to the Berlin Wall, a symbol of the Cold War.

Reagan was a rare world leader who was **beloved** by many of the people he touched worldwide. He is remembered as a positive influence on the world.

NAME: _____

Ronald Reagan

1. Below is a list of five events. (Circle) the **three** events that occurred as a **result** of Ronald Reagan's leadership.

The Berlin Wall is built in Germany.
The arms race begins.
A U.S. president visits Russia.
The U.S. ignores Russia.
The U.S. and Russia sign arms reduction treaties.

2. In your own words, explain how Ronald Reagan **ended** the arms race with Russia.

_____

_____

3. Reagan was well-liked worldwide. In **your opinion**, why do you think so many people liked Ronald Reagan? Your answer should be two to three sentences. Use examples from the passage to support your opinion.

_____

_____

_____

4. Ronald Reagan was known as a good speaker. He once said, **"All great change in America begins at the dinner table."** Describe what this quote means. Give examples from your own dinner table to support your explanation. Your answer should be two to three sentences.

_____

_____

_____

NAME: _____

Fidel Castro

1. **Write each word from the list beside its correct meaning. Use a dictionary to help you.**

embargo	hostile	personable	oppose
aid	dictator	isolated	

a) _____ Act against

b) _____ Well-liked

c) _____ Help

d) _____ A leader who rules with total power

e) _____ Separate from everyone else

f) _____ A government order that does not allow trade

g) _____ Angry towards

2. **The U.S. has an *embargo* against Cuba. What if your country had an embargo placed on it? Imagine what your country would be like if other countries would not trade with your country. Make a list of *five* things you could not have if your country was not allowed to trade.**

a) _____

b) _____

c) _____

d) _____

e) _____

3. **Locate Cuba on the map below. Next, locate the southernmost tip of Florida. Estimate the *distance* between Cuba and the U.S. Write your estimate in the box below.**

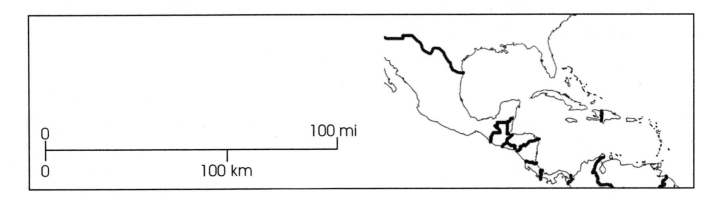

NAME: _____

Fidel Castro

F idel Castro became the leader of Cuba after leading the Cuban Revolution. He helped remove another leader from office during this **revolution**. After taking over the government, Castro has led Cuba for over forty years.

Cuba is a small island less than 100 miles from the southern tip of Florida. However, U.S. citizens are not allowed to travel to Cuba and the United States will not trade with Cuba. In fact, the U.S. has had an **embargo** against Cuba for over forty years.

Castro worked closely with Russian leaders until the end of the Cold War. Both countries had Communist governments. This was a serious threat to the United States.

U.S. leaders worried because they thought that Cuba would **aid** Russia in attack against the U.S. When the Cold War ended, Cuba and Russia ended their close relationship, but the relationship between the U.S. and Cuba remained openly **hostile**.

STOP

Why did U.S. leaders consider Cuba to be a serious threat?

_____

_____

People have many different opinions about Fidel Castro as a leader. Some people believe he is a **personable** leader. Other people believe he is a **dictator.** He has been accused of killing people who oppose him, but others consider Castro to be a hero.

Cuba remains somewhat **isolated** from the rest of the world. Cuba's **economy** has suffered since the end of the Cold War. They are now trying to attract tourists, but U.S. citizens still cannot travel to Cuba.

Fidel Castro

1. **Read the following four events. Write them in the correct order on the lines below, starting with the earliest event.**

   Castro works closely with Russia.
   Cuba encourages tourism.
   Castro takes over after the Cuban Revolution.
   Castro ends his close relationship with Russia.

   a) _____

   b) _____

   c) _____

   d) _____

2. **In your own words, explain why people have so many different *opinions* about Fidel Castro.**

   _____

   _____

   _____

3. **What do you think would happen if the U.S. *lifted* the embargo against Cuba?**

   _____

   _____

   _____

4. **Using the computers and other resources in your classroom, find *four facts* about Cuba. List those facts on the lines provided below.**

   a) _____

   b) _____

   c) _____

   d) _____

Vicente Fox

1. **Read the definitions on the left. Find the correct definition on the right. Write the correct letter on the line provided. You may use a dictionary to help you.**

a		_____
b		_____
c		_____
d	stabilize	_____
e	immigration	_____
f		_____

A Not firm or strict

B

C

D

E

F To keep from changing

2. **The map has arrows pointing at three countries: the United States, Cuba, and Mexico. Using colored pencils, follow the directions below.**

   a) Color the United States **red.**   b) Color Cuba **blue.**   c) Color Mexico **green.**

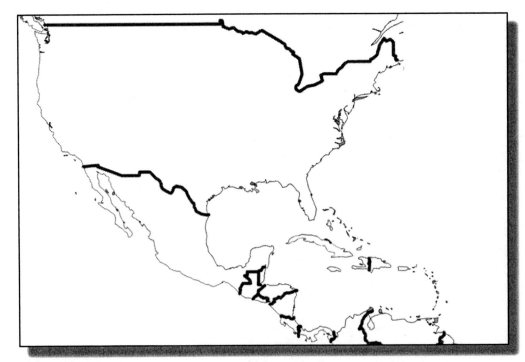

Vicente Fox

Vicente Fox was the 72nd President of Mexico. He was born on July 2, 1942 in Mexico City, but he grew up on a ranch in the country. He moved back to the city when he attended college.

Vicente Fox did not start out wanting to be a politician. After he finished college, Fox started working for Coca-Cola. He started at the bottom, and then was put in charge of **operations** in Mexico. Eventually, he was in charge of Coca-Cola's operations in all of Latin America.

When Fox became President, he decided to fix the problems he saw in the Mexican government. Mexico had the reputation of being **corrupt** and too **lax** on drugs. Fox worked to stop corruption within the Mexican government. He also helped create new laws that made it harder to buy and sell drugs.

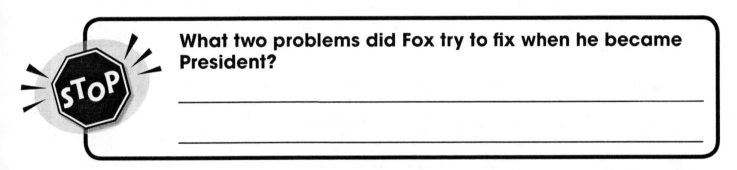

What two problems did Fox try to fix when he became President?

_____

_____

Before Fox took office, Mexico was not very involved in world politics. They had a strict rule that said Mexico should not criticize how other governments decide to run their countries. Fox decided to increase Mexico's involvement in world politics.

Fox worked with the U.S. to try to control open **immigration** between the Mexico-U.S. borders. George W. Bush supported these discussions, but no new laws were passed in the U.S.

Fox also worked with other Latin American countries. Mexico held several international **summits** to talk about global issues. Guests included Fidel Castro and George W. Bush. The two leaders were not in the same room at the same time, but Fox wanted to help the two leaders work together.

Vicente Fox

1. Below is a list of five events. (Circle) the *three* events that occurred as a result of Vicente Fox's leadership.

   Fox works with both Bush and Castro.

   Mexico becomes less involved in world politics.

   The U.S and Mexico talk about immigration.

   It is harder to buy and sell drugs in Mexico.

2. Answer each question below in a complete sentence.

   a) What company did Fox work for before he became a politician?

   _____

   b) What was Mexico's opinion about being involved in world politics before Fox?

   _____

   c) Why did Fox try to work with George W. Bush?

   _____

3. Mexico and the United States share a large border. Do you think the border should be *open?* This would mean that people would be able to travel back and forth whenever they want. Your answer should be two to three sentences.

   _____

   _____

   _____

   _____

NAME: _____

Juan and Eva Peron

1. **Write each word from the list beside its correct meaning. Use a dictionary to help you.**

eliminate	recognized	ambitious
fled	wealthy	organization
linked		

a) _____ Group

b) _____ To get rid of

c) _____ Connected

d) _____ Rich

e) _____ Ran away from

f) _____ Noticed as

g) _____ Wanting

2. **The Perons worked hard in order to try to help the poor people of their country. List *five* ways in which your country could help its poor people.**

a) _____

b) _____

c) _____

d) _____

e) _____

Juan and Eva Peron

Juan   Eva Peron

Juan Peron was a three time President of Argentina. His wife, Eva, was a powerful leader who worked with her husband. They are still very popular figures in Argentina today.

Before he became President, Juan was a colonel in the military, Minister of War, and Vice-President of Argentina. The Perons had several goals that they worked towards together during his Presidency. They wanted to **eliminate** poverty. They also wanted to give power to the working class. Their goals angered the **wealthy** people who did not want to see the working class get richer.

STOP

Why were the wealthy people of Argentina unhappy with the Perons?

_____

_____

_____

Eva Peron was one of the most powerful women of her time. She was **recognized** as a leader within her husband's **organization**. Eva was a very **ambitious** woman. She traveled to Europe on the "Rainbow Tour". On the tour, she met with many European leaders.

When Juan Peron ran for a second time, Eva wanted to be his Vice-President. The military was against the idea of a woman as Vice-President. Besides, Eva quickly became too sick for the job. She died shortly after her husband won the election.

Juan and Eva Peron were **controversial** leaders. Many people loved them. Other people accused them of spending too much money. The Perons have also been **linked** to former Nazis. Many former Nazis **fled** to Argentina.

Juan and Eva Peron

1. The Perons worked hard to improve the lives of people in Argentina. List the *two* goals the Perons worked together to achieve.

   a) _____

   b) _____

2. Describe the *purpose* of the "Rainbow Tour". Answer in a complete sentence.

   _____

   _____

3. Eva Peron wanted to be the Vice-President of Argentina. In your own words, explain the *two* reasons why Eva could not have the job. Your answer should be three to four sentences.

   _____

   _____

   _____

   _____

4. Would you vote for a woman to lead your country? Why or why not? Answer in a complete sentence.

   _____

   _____

   _____

 Before You Read   NAME: _____

Margaret Thatcher

1. Complete each sentence with a word from the list. Use a dictionary to help you.

allies	apartheid	published
negotiated	release	

a) We watched the zookeeper _____ the lion from the cage.

b) The book was _____ a year later.

c) People were upset by _____ and wanted everyone to be treated equally.

d) Canada and the United States are _____.

e) A new deal was _____ between the two boys.

---

2. Using the resources in your classroom, list the *four countries* in the United Kingdom.

a) _____
    _____

b) _____
    _____

c) _____
    _____

d) _____
    _____

3. On the map below, *label* the four countries that are the United Kingdom.

Margaret Thatcher

Margaret Thatcher was the Prime Minister of the United Kingdom for over ten years. She was the first woman Prime Minister. She is called "The Iron Lady of British Politics" because she was known for being strong and intelligent.

Thatcher often worked closely with Ronald Reagan. The two leaders were **allies** on many international issues. Thatcher helped end the Cold War. She **negotiated** talks with Reagan and the leader of Russia. She helped bring the two leaders together to work out their differences.

She was also interested in other global issues. Thatcher invited leaders from South Africa to talk about ending **apartheid.** She tried to convince the leaders to **release** Nelson Mandela from prison. They did not listen to her advice.

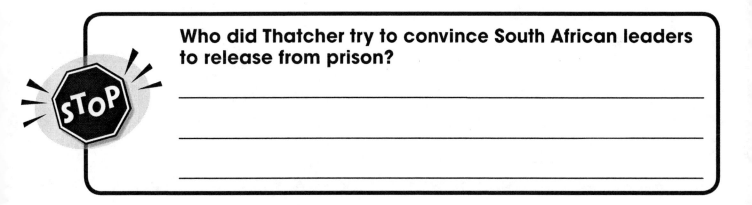

Who did Thatcher try to convince South African leaders to release from prison?

_____

_____

_____

Before she became a politician, Margaret Thatcher was a **chemist.** She helped invent the first soft-serve ice cream. She became involved in saving the environment because of her love of science. She was one of the first world leaders to talk about global warming and acid rain.

Margaret Thatcher has remained active in world politics since leaving office. She has also **published** several books discussing her opinions on world politics.

NAME: _____

Margaret Thatcher

1. **Complete each question below in a complete sentence.**

   a) How did Margaret Thatcher help end the **Cold War?**

   _____

   _____

   b) What were the **two** reasons why Thatcher met with South African leaders?

   _____

   _____

2. Margaret Thatcher worked to help the environment. Choose either **global warming** or **acid rain.** Use the resources in your classroom to learn **five facts** about the issue you have chosen.

   a) _____

   b) _____

   c) _____

   d) _____

   e) _____

3. Thatcher once said, **"You may have to fight a battle more than once to win it."** In two to three sentences, describe a time when you had to keep trying in order to reach a goal.

   _____

   _____

   _____

Mikhail Gorbachev

1. **Write each word from the list beside its correct meaning. Use a dictionary to help you.**

collapsed	goods	coup	citizens	shortage

_____ **a)** Items that can be purchased

_____ **b)** Forceful takeover

_____ **c)** Not enough

_____ **d)** Fell apart

_____ **e)** People who live in a country

2. **List *three* facts you have already learned about the Cold War.**

a) _____

b) _____

c) _____

3. **Russia is one of the countries that were involved in the Cold War. You have read about three other countries also involved in the Cold War. Name the *three* other countries below.**

a) _____

b) _____

c) _____

Reading Passage

NAME: _____

Mikhail Gorbachev

Mikhail Gorbachev was the last leader of the Soviet Union (Russia) before it **collapsed**. He was also the first elected President of the Soviet Union.

Gorbachev worked with Reagan and Thatcher to end the Cold War. He developed close relationships with both leaders. Gorbachev and Reagan met many times to **eliminate** many nuclear weapons. This helped end the arms race and the Cold War.

Gorbachev wanted to improve the lives of his citizens. He allowed freedom of speech, which was against the law before. He allowed people to open and own their own businesses. Before he made this change, businesses and stores were owned by the government.

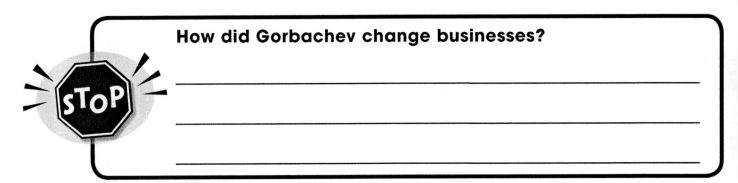

How did Gorbachev change businesses?

_____

_____

_____

He also held the first election in his country since the Cold War. He was voted the first President of the Soviet Union.

Gorbachev also opened his country to Western goods. This allowed free trade and let people have more choices. He helped to end food **shortages** and gave his people greater freedom. People decided that they liked having choices. They wanted even more freedom. This led to the collapse of his country.

Mikhail Gorbachev left the government after a **coup.** He is now very active in environmental issues. He was given the Nobel Peace Prize because of his efforts to improve his country and the world.

Mikhail Gorbachev

1. (Circle) the word **TRUE** if the statement is TRUE **or** (Circle) the word **FALSE** if it is FALSE.

a) Gorbachev worked with Castro to help end the Cold War.
  TRUE   FALSE

b) Gorbachev worked with Reagan to eliminate some nuclear weapons.
  TRUE   FALSE

c) Gorbachev did not allow citizens to own their own businesses.
  TRUE   FALSE

d) Freedom of speech was made legal.
  TRUE   FALSE

e) Gorbachev is still active in environmental issues.

  TRUE   FALSE

2. In your own words, **summarize** how people in Russia reacted to their new freedoms.

_____

_____

_____

_____

3. Mikhail Gorbachev once said, **"If not me, who? And if not now, when?"** In your opinion, what does this quote say about Gorbachev as a person? Your answer should be two to three sentences.

_____

_____

_____

_____

Nelson Mandela

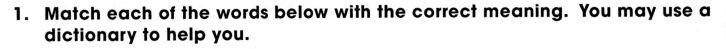

1. **Match each of the words below with the correct meaning. You may use a dictionary to help you.**

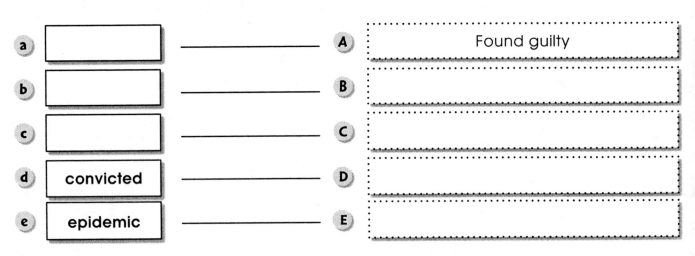

a			**A**	Found guilty
b			**B**	
c			**C**	
d	convicted		**D**	
e	epidemic		**E**	

2. Nelson Mandela fought his country's government. He wanted to allow everyone the right to vote. List **two** reasons why it is important to vote.

a) _____

b) _____

3. Imagine that you were not allowed to vote in your country because of your **race.** Describe how that would make you feel. Give one reason to support your answer.

_____

_____

_____

_____

NAME: _____

Nelson Mandela

Nelson Mandela was the 11th President of South Africa. He is most famous for being a political **activist.** He worked to end **apartheid.**

The South African government did not allow equal rights for all of their citizens. Mandela began fighting with the **resistance** against the racism he saw. He was arrested twice. He was first put in jail for **treason.** He was arrested for voicing his opinions. He was found not guilty.

What was Mandela arrested for the first time?

_____

_____

_____

He was arrested a second time. This time, he was **convicted** of organizing an armed attack against the government. He spent twenty-seven years in prison for standing up for what he believed.

His story was famous, and eventually people from around the world put pressure on South Africa. The people of the world wanted Mandela to be freed. The government had to give him his freedom.

After getting out of prison, Mandela made bringing peace to his country his main focus. He worked to give everyone the right to vote. His hard work paid off. He was the first President of South Africa to win an election open to all citizens.

Mandela worked with many human rights groups after he left office. He also worked to fight the AIDS **epidemic** in Africa. He has received the Nobel Peace Prize for his efforts to help end apartheid in South Africa.

Nelson Mandela

1. Place the following events on the timeline below.

Events:

a) The world pressures South Africa to free Mandela.

b) Mandela works to stop the AIDS epidemic.

c) Nelson Mandela is convicted and serves twenty-seven years.

d) Mandela is found not guilty of treason.

e) Mandela is elected the 11th President of South Africa.

2. Nelson Mandela once said, **"Education is the most powerful weapon which you can use to change the world."** Explain what this quote means in your own words.

_____

_____

_____

3. How would you **improve** race relations in South Africa? List **three** suggestions.

a) _____

b) _____

c) _____

Indira Gandhi

1. **Complete each sentence with a word from the list. Use a dictionary to help you.**

surplus	threat	assassinate
export	fraud	

a) Mexico will _____ their fruit and sell it to other countries.

b) It is against the law to _____ a country's leader.

c) Mom made a _____ to take away my computer if my grades do not improve.

d) We have a _____ of tomatoes, so we are giving them to our friends.

e) Because of her earlier _____, I did not believe her when she was telling the truth.

2. Indira Gandhi decided to focus on the problems facing her country. If you were the leader of your country, what **three** problems would you focus on? List them below.

a) _____

b) _____

c) _____

3. Select **one** of the problems you listed above. In a sentence, describe one way you would try to **solve** the problem.

_____

_____

_____

Indira Gandhi

I ndira Gandhi was elected the Prime Minister of India two times. Her father, Jawaharlal Nehru, was the Prime Minister years before she became India's leader. She was one of the first women to be an elected leader of a country.

India was in very bad shape when Gandhi took over as leader. She decided to focus on her country rather than global concerns. India was a very poor country and there was not enough food for everyone in the country. Gandhi helped turn a food **shortage** in India into a food **surplus.** India started to **export** their surplus to other countries to make money.

Gandhi started building more nuclear weapons. She thought that both China and Pakistan were **threats** to India. Problems between India and Pakistan became very bad. Gandhi led an eleven-month war against Pakistan. The war ended when Russia helped India and Pakistan reach a peaceful agreement.

STOP

Why did Gandhi start building nuclear weapons?

_____

_____

_____

During Gandhi's leadership, she worked well with Russian leaders. She also met with leaders from the United States, United Kingdom, and Bangladesh.

Indira Gandhi was thought by some people to have committed election **fraud.** A religious group wanted her to step down. She had her army attack the Golden Temple. This is the religious group's holiest place of worship.

This angered the religious group even more. She was **assassinated** by two of her guards who were members of this group. She is remembered for improving the quality of life for Indian citizens.

NAME: _____

Indira Gandhi

1. Indira Gandhi was a leader who worked in the best interest of her country. Use the reading passage to find **two** examples that show Gandhi had India's best interests at heart.

   a) _____

   _____

   b) _____

   _____

2. In your own words, explain why Indira Gandhi was **assassinated.** Your answer should be three to four sentences.

   _____

   _____

   _____

   _____

   _____

3. What choice would you make if you were Indira Gandhi? Would you choose to leave your job, or would you stay and fight? Give one reason to support your answers.

   _____

   _____

   _____

   _____

   _____

NAME: _____

Yasser Arafat

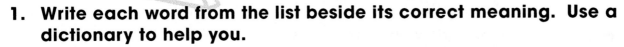

1. **Write each word from the list beside its correct meaning. Use a dictionary to help you.**

figure	rightfully	hostage	liberation	notable

a) _____ Belonging to

b) _____ Freedom

c) _____ A person held against their wishes by another person

d) _____ A well-known person

e) _____ Famous

2. **On the map below, find Israel and Palestine on the map. Using your colored pencils, follow these directions.**

a) Color Palestine **blue.**

b) Color Israel **green.**

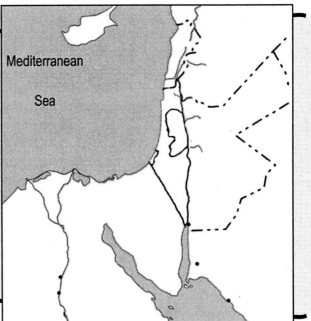

3. **Using the resources in your classroom, write down *four facts* about Israel.**

a) _____

b) _____

c) _____

d) _____

NAME: _____

Yasser Arafat

Yasser Arafat is a controversial **figure** in world politics. Some people believe he is freedom fighter. Other people believe that he is a terrorist.

Arafat first received the world's attention because of his connection to the PLO, or the Palestine **Liberation** Organization. This is a group that wanted to force the Jewish people out of Israel. The PLO believed that Israel was **rightfully** part of Palestine. They wanted Israel returned to Palestine.

Why did the PLO want Israel returned to Palestine?

_____

_____

_____

The PLO was involved in several acts of terrorism. One of the most **notable** happened at the Munich Olympics. At the Olympics, terrorists stormed Olympic village and killed two Israeli athletes. Then, they kidnapped nine other athletes and held them as **hostages.** They wanted 200 Palestinian prisoners released from Israeli prisons. The nine Israeli athletes were killed.

Yasser Arafat was a leader in the PLO at the time of the Munich Olympics. He was **linked** to other terrorist activities through the years. However, as he got older, Arafat decided to work for peace.

Arafat worked with leaders from the U.S. and Israel on a peace agreement. The agreement helped end the fighting between Israel and Palestine.

Many people now saw Arafat as a leader who was interested in world peace. He was awarded the Nobel Peace Prize because of the peace agreement he signed with Israel.

Yasser Arafat

1. In your own words, explain why people had different **opinions** about Yasser Arafat. Use one example from the passage to support your answer.

_____

_____

_____

2. Arafat once said, **"I come bearing an olive branch in one hand, and the freedom fighter's gun in the other. Do not let the olive branch fall from my hand."**

What **conclusions** can you draw about Arafat's state of mind at the time? In other words, how did he feel about his decision?

_____

_____

_____

3. Imagine the peace agreement between Palestine and Israel had never been signed. **Predict** how the world would be different if the agreement had never happened.

_____

_____

_____

4. Arafat completely changed his approach. Why do you think Arafat chose to work peacefully?

_____

_____

_____

NAME: _____

Jiang Zemin

1. **Match each of the words below with the correct meaning. You may use a dictionary to help you.**

a		_____	**A**	Country
b		_____	**B**	
c		_____	**C**	
d	Nation	_____	**D**	
e	Standard	_____	**E**	

2. China's Jiang Zemin was a Communist leader. Identify **two** other Communist leaders you have learned about previously.

   a) _____

   b) _____

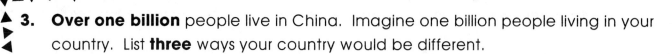

3. **Over one billion** people live in China. Imagine one billion people living in your country. List **three** ways your country would be different.

   a) _____

   _____

   b) _____

   _____

   c) _____

   _____

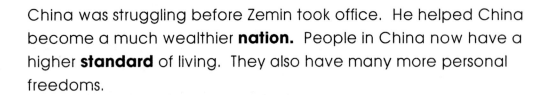
Jiang Zemin

Jiang Zemin served as a leader of the Communist Party in China for several **decades.** His different leadership **roles** include General Secretary of the Communist Party, President of the People's Republic of China, and Chairman of the Central Military **Commission.**

China was struggling before Zemin took office. He helped China become a much wealthier **nation.** People in China now have a higher **standard** of living. They also have many more personal freedoms.

One major change Zemin led changed politics in China. He allowed private business owners to be members of the Communist Party. This allowed more people to become directly involved with the government.

STOP

How did Zemin change politics in China?

_____

_____

_____

_____

Zemin became very involved in world politics. He spoke several **foreign** languages and liked learning about different cultures. China's relationships with other countries improved.

Zemin visited the U.S. and spoke with President Clinton. Clinton later visited Zemin in China. Before this happened, China and the U.S. had a difficult relationship.

Zemin also brought China into the World Trade Organization. This also helped China become more involved in the world.

China got Hong Kong and Macao back from England and Portugal during Zemin's **term**. He **negotiated** with European leaders to give ownership back to China. He also put in a successful bid for China to host the Summer Olympics before he left office.

NAME: _____

Jiang Zemin

1. List the **three** political jobs held by Jiang Zemin.

    a) _____

    b) _____

    c) _____

2. Five changes are listed below. Four are changes made by Zemin. Circle the **four** changes by Jiang Zemin.

   China will host the Summer Olympics.
   Private business owners can participate in the Communist party.
   The relationship between the US and China improves.
   Hong Kong and Macao are turned over to European countries.
   China becomes involved in the World Trade Organization

3. Jiang Zemin was one of the first Chinese leaders to talk with the media. Imagine you are a reporter. List **four questions** you would ask Zemin about his career.

    a) _____

    b) _____

    c) _____

    d) _____

4. Think about the **changes** made by Jiang Zemin. Why did these changes make China a better, stronger country? Your answer should be two to three sentences.

    _____

    _____

    _____

The Dalai Lama

1. **Write each word from the list beside its correct meaning. Use a dictionary to help you.**

> reincarnated   asylum   waste   groomed   restore

a) _____   To bring back

b) _____   Scraps or leftovers

c) _____   Brought back to life in another body

d) _____   A safe place

e) _____   Made ready for

2. **The map shows both China and Tibet. Use your colored pencils to follow the directions.**

   a) Color Tibet **Red.**

   b) Color China **green.**

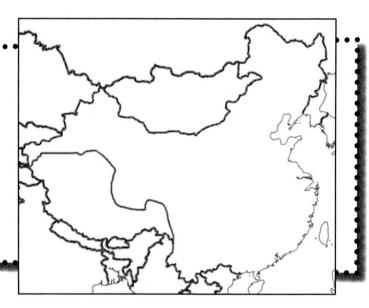

3. *Three* other world leaders you have read about have been awarded the *Nobel Peace Prize.* List the names of those three leaders below.

   a) _____

   b) _____

   c) _____

 Reading Passage

The Dalai Lama

Tenzin Gyatso is the 14th Dalai Lama. He is the head of state and spiritual leader of Tibet. The Dalai Lama is also called His Holiness. He is the main leader of the Buddhist religion.

The Dalai Lama was discovered to be the **reincarnated** spirit of the last Dalai Lama at the age of two. He was **groomed** to be the Dalai Lama during his childhood.

How did Tenzin Gyatso become the Dalai Lama?

STOP

_____

_____

_____

He took over as the Dalai Lama after Chinese soldiers invaded Tibet. The Dalai Lama tried to work out a peaceful solution with China. He was not successful. His Holiness had to **flee** to India where he was given political **asylum.**

The Dalai Lama worked to get his country back from China. He went to the United Nations for help. This was not successful either.

The Five Point Peace Plan was created by the Dalai Lama. He wanted to establish Tibet as a free zone. He wanted to **restore** personal freedoms taken away by the Chinese invaders. He wanted to stop the building of nuclear weapons in Tibet. China was dumping nuclear **waste** in Tibet, and the Dalai Lama wanted that to end. He also wanted to open discussions about freeing Tibet.

China did not agree to the plan. However, the Dalai Lama was **recognized** for his efforts. He was awarded the Nobel Peace Prize for his work to free Tibet and help people around the world.

NAME: _____

The Dalai Lama

1. The Dalai Lama created a Five Point Peace Plan in order to work peacefully with China. List the five points below.

   a) _____

   b) _____

   c) _____

   d) _____

   e) _____

2. Why do you think Dalai Lamas are found when they are children? Explain your opinion in two to three sentences.

   _____

   _____

   _____

3. How would you design a peace plan with China? List **two original points** your plan would include.

   a) _____

   b) _____

4. The Dalai Lama cannot safely return to his country. Describe how you would feel if you could not return to your country. Describe how you would handle the situation. Your answer should be two to three sentences.

   _____

   _____

   _____

Writing Tasks

1. Think about what you have learned about Ronald Reagan, Margaret Thatcher, and Mikhail Gorbachev. Use the Compare and Contrast Pyramid found on page 44. Describe how the leaders are different from each other in the outside triangles. Explain how they are similar in the inside pyramid. Use the graphic organizer in order to write a four paragraph essay.

2. Imagine what the world would be like if The Cold War did not end. Write a four paragraph description of how you think the world would be different.

3. Select one of the countries you have just studied. Write a one-page research paper about your country, including the capital, government, agriculture, industry, and history. You may use the Internet and library to help you.

4. Yasser Arafat worked to end fighting in the Middle East, but his plan did not work for long. Write a one-page peace plan for the Middle East. Include any ideas you have for ending the violence and getting leaders together to talk.

5. Use the Snapshots Organizer on page 46 to summarize the Perons' rise to power. Use supporting details from the reading passage to help you. Your summary should be one to two paragraphs.

6. Several of the leaders you have learned about made decisions that changed their country and the world. Select one leader you have studied. Evaluate their decisions and choices. Do you agree with their decisions? Would you have made the same choices?

Hands-On Activity # 2

Compare and Contrast Pyramid

Using the Pyramid below, describe how Reagan, Thatcher, and Gorbachev are similar to and different from each other.

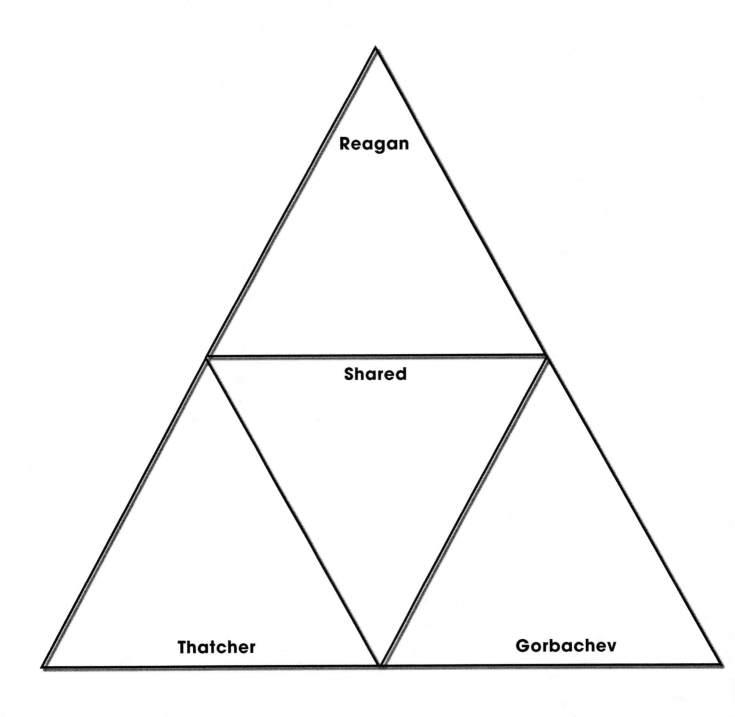

Snapshots Organizer

List the steps taken by the Perons, in the proper order, to achieve and keep power. Write one step in each snapshot below.

NAME: _____

Crossword Puzzle!

Across

1. The first President of the Soviet Union

3. U.S. President who helped end Cold War

7. U.S. President who declared a war on terrorism

9. Argentinian leader who worked to help poor

10. Spiritual leader of Tibet

12. In prison for over 20 years for what he believed

13. Made drug laws stricter in Mexico

Down

1. Worked to improve conditions in India

2. Close ally with Russian leaders during Cold War

4. Weapons

6. To let go

7. Made ready for

8. Chinese leader who helped China become more involved in World Politics

10. Known as "The Iron Lady" in the United Kingdom

11. A former leader of the PLO who worked for

Word List

Gorbachev	Castro	Vincente Fox
Zemin	Juan Peron	arms
George W. Bush	Gandhi	Ronald Reagan
groomed	The Dalai Lama	Thatcher
release	Arafat	

NAME: _____

Word Search

Find all of the words in the Word Search. Words are written horizontally, vertically, diagonally, and some are even written backwards.

t	e	r	t	f	u	i	s	o	l	a	t	e	d	i	y	d	a
e	e	b	k	c	o	n	f	l	i	c	t	w	i	h	t	k	p
r	u	r	a	r	g	y	v	d	m	g	c	k	a	n	i	c	a
m	y	t	r	e	a	s	o	n	g	j	b	e	a	l	k	a	r
r	g	n	h	o	s	f	d	e	c	a	d	e	w	t	t	j	t
l	o	a	w	s	r	h	o	w	t	m	h	a	d	h	p	h	h
i	t	l	a	e	g	i	t	e	g	o	y	j	f	d	u	g	e
d	k	l	d	g	j	s	s	n	s	u	m	m	i	t	r	i	i
e	r	i	f	e	u	v	c	t	w	f	t	j	d	l	r	h	d
l	k	e	h	l	q	e	a	d	c	o	u	r	s	e	o	t	i
f	c	s	p	d	w	g	z	x	t	u	s	c	h	p	c	w	e
a	f	r	x	m	e	x	p	o	r	t	h	q	e	i	l	d	t
c	u	r	e	c	o	n	o	m	y	h	u	e	t	q	e	i	k
s	c	r	o	w	t	o	j	d	r	y	c	i	g	k	w	r	e
t	h	r	e	a	t	e	a	e	y	u	z	p	n	l	o	h	e
w	d	u	g	l	s	r	s	h	g	e	p	i	d	e	m	i	c
a	o	j	i	a	d	g	u	k	n	v	l	n	r	m	y	e	l
l	y	g	e	e	a	d	u	s	c	z	f	i	m	o	n	f	k
s	k	l	s	w	e	a	l	t	h	y	u	i	s	s	r	h	s
n	e	r	y	e	g	k	y	f	a	d	i	k	j	d	e	e	e
r	r	l	i	b	e	r	a	t	i	o	n	a	r	g	o	y	s
i	f	y	r	t	p	e	r	s	o	n	a	b	l	e	u	o	i
r	e	i	n	c	a	r	n	a	t	e	d	k	f	g	y	e	g

terrorist	summit	reincarnated	release
term	aid	export	threat
hostage	corrupt	conflict	economy
treason	epidemic	fled	goods
apartheid	linked	allies	wealthy
isolated	surplus	highjack	personable
citizens	decade	course	liberation

NAME: _____

Comprehension Quiz

25

Part A

5

1. Circle the word **TRUE** if the statement is TRUE **or** Circle the word **FALSE** if it is FALSE.

a) Yasser Arafat always worked for peace in the Middle East.

TRUE   **FALSE**

b) China has allowed the Dalai Lama to return to Tibet to lead.

TRUE   **FALSE**

c) Thatcher, Reagan, and Gorbachev worked to end the Cold War.

TRUE   **FALSE**

d) Indira Gandhi created a food shortage in India.

TRUE   **FALSE**

e) Mandela helped apartheid spread in South Africa.

TRUE   **FALSE**

Part B

Match the leader on the left with their actions on the right.

5

1   

A   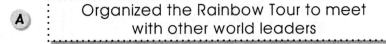
Organized the Rainbow Tour to meet with other world leaders

2   

B   

3   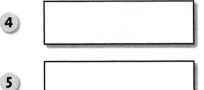

C

4

D

5

E

SUBTOTAL: /10

After You Read 📖

Comprehension Quiz

Part C

Answer the questions in complete sentences.

1. Explain how **Reagan** helped end the Cold War. Give examples when answering.

_____

_____

_____

2. Explain how **Eva Peron** was different from other women leaders. Give examples when answering.

_____

_____

_____

3. Explain how **Zemin** helped China become more involved in world politics. Give examples when answering.

_____

_____

_____

4. Explain why people have different opinions on **Yasser Arafat**. Give examples when answering.

_____

_____

_____

5. Why did the **Dalai Lama** create the Five Point Peace Plan? Give two examples when answering.

_____

_____

_____

SUBTOTAL: **/15**

NAME: _____

History of the Voting System

1. **Match each of the words below with the correct meaning. You may use a dictionary to help you.**

    a [　　　　　　] _____ A : A government by the people :

    b [　　　　　　] _____ B : :

    c [　　　　　　] _____ C : :

    d [election] _____ D : :

    e [democratic] _____ E : :

    f [　　　　　　] _____ F : A choice :

2. **Voting is an important part of being a citizen. List three reasons why it is important to vote.**

    a) _____

    b) _____

    _____

3. **There are several countries in the world where people are not allowed to vote. This could be because of their race, religion, or gender. Do you believe this is fair? Answer in two to three complete sentences.**

    _____

    _____

    _____

    _____

History of the Voting System

Voting is an important part of a democratic government. It is a way for the people to choose between a number of different options. Voting can be used in everyday life in order to make decisions. Voting is used in elections because it allows the people to select the leaders they believe in most.

Voting has been used by governments for thousands of years. It is believed that voting was first created by the ancient Greeks in the 6th century B.C. There are no exact records, but most experts believe voting starting around 508 B.C.

In ancient Greece, only male landowners could vote. This means that there were very few votes. These votes were written on broken pots and then counted. This way of voting was also used to choose leaders in ancient India, Pakistan, and Afghanistan.

How did ancient Greeks vote?

_____

_____

In medieval Venice, a new form of voting was created in the 13th century. This new type of voting is called "approval voting". In this system, voters cast a vote for every choice they feel is acceptable. They do not vote for people they do not like.

Medieval Venetians elected representatives to the Great Council. This group had forty members. This was one of the models for the parliamentary system of government.

NAME: _____

History of the Voting System

Voting requirements have changed quite a bit throughout history. Not every person has been allowed to vote. Many countries only allowed male land owners to vote. Other countries did not allow people who were not white to vote.

The United States was one of those countries. African-American citizens were not allowed to vote until 1860. There are still some countries in the world where not every citizen is allowed to vote because of their race or religion.

Around the world, women have not always been able to vote. Canada only allowed women to vote in three provinces in 1916. Other provinces followed in the next few years. In the United States, women got the right to vote in 1920.

Other countries have been slow to allow women to vote. Switzerland did not allow women to vote until the 1970's. Several countries in the Middle East still do not allow women to vote. Saudi Arabia is one of those countries.

There are a few international groups that work to protect voting rights around the world. They work to make sure that everyone who has the right to vote can vote freely. They also work to try to gain voting rights for all citizens so that all the people can vote, not just a few.

Two of these groups, the United Nations Fair Elections Commissions and the Carter Center, have been very active in helping elections in foreign countries remain safe.

Voting Line, Iraq

NAME: _____

History of the Voting System

1. Circle if the word **TRUE** if the statement is TRUE **or** Circle the word **FALSE** if it is FALSE.

   a) Voting was created by the ancient Romans.

   TRUE   **FALSE**

   b) Voting allows the people to choose their leaders.

   TRUE   **FALSE**

   c) Switzerland was the first country to let women vote.

   TRUE   **FALSE**

   d) Every country allows all their citizens to vote.

   TRUE   **FALSE**

   e) Medieval Venetians elected members to the Great Council.

   TRUE   **FALSE**

   f) The Carter Center helps elections around the world.

   TRUE   **FALSE**

---

2. Circle the event that happened first.

   a)   Greeks voted using broken pieces of pots.
        Venetians used approval voting.

   b)   Women had the right to vote in Saudi Arabia.
        Women had the right to vote in Canada.

---

3. **The medieval Venetians created approval voting. In your own words, summarize how approval voting works. Your answer should be two to three sentences.**

   _____

   _____

   _____

   _____

History of the Voting System

4. Imagine you could interview a woman in Saudi Arabia who is not allowed to vote in her country's elections. List three questions you would ask her about this topic.

a) _____

b) _____

c) _____

5. If you were a leader in a country like Saudi Arabia that did not allow women to vote, would you change this? Your explanation should be at least two to three sentences.

_____

_____

_____

_____

_____

_____

NAME: _____

The Legitimacy of Democratic Government

1. **Complete each sentence with a word from the list. Use a dictionary to help you.**

violate	citizens	democracy
representatives	persecution	

a) The _____ are elected by the people.

b) If you _____ the rules, you will be grounded.

c) A _____ is a government for the people.

d) The people who live in an area or country are the _____.

e) Many people have left their own country because of _____.

2. **Using the resources in your classroom, list five countries that are democracies.**

a) _____

b) _____

c) _____

d) _____

e) _____

3. **Now use your classroom resources to list three countries that are not democracies.**

a) _____

b) _____

c) _____

The Legitimacy of Democratic Government

Democracy means rule of the people. It describes a government where the people who live in that country choose their representatives. These representatives are chosen in an election and represent the citizens when making decisions for the good of the community or country.

How are representatives chosen in a democracy?

_____

_____

_____

In a democracy, all citizens should be seen as equal by the government. This means that every citizen should have the right to vote, no matter their race, religion, or beliefs. Every citizen has the right to vote in a true democracy.

Ancient Greeks in Athens were the first to have a democracy. However, slaves and women were not able to vote. Since the majority of the people living in Athens were slaves or not citizens, very few people were allowed to vote. Democracy in ancient Greece did not last long for this reason.

Other ancient cultures had democratic governments, but not all of the people were allowed to vote. These ancient cultures include India, Rome, Pakistan, and the Iroquois tribe in North America. However, the Iroquois only allowed the oldest females of the family to elect and remove leaders.

The Legitimacy of Democratic Government

A democracy should also protect the human rights of all its citizens. This means that people can speak freely and express their opinions without fear of persecution. Democracies allow people to read and study whatever they want. They can also vote for whoever they want during elections.

If someone is arrested in a democracy, they will receive a fair trial. They will have an opportunity to present their case to the court and will receive a fair judgment. They will not be put in prison unfairly and without good reason.

Many countries in the world, including the United States, Canada, the United Kingdom, and India are democracies. They allow their citizens to elect their representatives, protect their freedoms, and protect their basic human rights.

Many other countries also claim to be democracies. However, they are not true democracies. One reason may be because they either do not allow all of their citizens to vote. Bhutan and Saudi Arabia do not allow all citizens to vote.

Another reason may be because they violate some of the idea of a true democracy. Some countries say they are democracies, but they do not allow people full freedom.

For example, they may not allow people to express their opinions without having to suffer a penalty. They also may not allow people to read certain books or study certain subjects.

For these reasons, international groups are working to help the people in these countries get basic human rights through democracy.

The Legitimacy of Democratic Government

1. **Below is a list of six ideas. Circle the four ideas that are democratic ideas.**

   Protects human rights

   Allows only land owners to vote

   Does not allow people to study other governments

   All citizens can vote

   Protects the freedoms of its citizens

   People are allowed to express their opinions freely

2. **The ancient Greeks were the first to have a democratic government. Explain how the democracy of ancient Greece is different from true democracies now. Your answer should be one to two complete sentences.**

   _____

   _____

3. **Explain why democracy failed in ancient Greece. Your answer should be one to two sentences.**

   _____

   _____

   _____

4. **Compare the Iroquois democracy to other democracies at that time. Tell how they are alike and different. Your answer should be three to four sentences.**

   _____

   _____

   _____

   _____

The Legitimacy of Democratic Government

5. **Democracy spread quickly in the 20th century. Predict how democracy will change in the 21st century. Your answer should be three to four complete sentences.**

_____

_____

_____

_____

_____

_____

_____

6. **Do you believe a democracy represents the people? State your opinion in three to four complete sentences.**

_____

_____

_____

_____

_____

_____

_____

_____

NAME: _____

Presidential System of Government

1. **Write each word from the list next to the correct meaning. Use a dictionary to help you.**

term	bill	cabinet
legislature	veto	

a) A group of people that make laws _____.

b) The power of a president to stop a law _____.

c) The first draft of a law _____.

d) The president's group of advisors _____.

e) A period of time _____.

2. **Many governments follow the presidential system of government. List five countries that have presidents as their leaders. Use the resources in your classroom to help you.**

a) _____

b) _____

c) _____

d) _____

e) _____

3. **Being president can be a challenge. Imagine you are the president of your country. Identify three issues you would address if you were president.**

a) _____

b) _____

c) _____

Presidential System of Government

The presidential system of government is a government ruled by a president who won a national election. The president is both the head of state and the head of the government.

The president is elected by the people in a free election. Each government has a fixed presidential term of several years. The most common term is four years. During this time, the president acts as a representative of the people who elected him when meeting with foreign representatives and making important decisions.

In most governments that use the presidential system, the president cannot introduce bills to the legislature. However, there is one exception. In Puerto Rico, the president can introduce a bill. This does not usually occur in other countries that follow the presidential system of government.

The president also cannot vote in the legislature on bills or other issues. If the president does not agree with a bill passed by the legislature, the president can veto the bill. When the president vetoes a bill, the bill is sent back to the legislature to be approved or not approved. If the bill does not receive enough support from the legislature at this point, the bill dies. If the bill does get enough support, it becomes a law.

Why does a president veto a bill?

_____

_____

NAME: _____

Presidential System of Government

The White House, Washington USA

The presidential system of government does not allow one part of government to become more powerful than another. The president does not have complete power because he cannot make laws. The legislature does not have the power to carry out laws. Both parts of the government work separately to make the best decisions for their representatives.

Most presidents have a group of experts who give them advice. This group is called a cabinet. When making important decisions, the president usually gets the advice of the cabinet before making a final decision. The president does not have to follow the advice of his cabinet, but does consider the advice when making a decision.

Presidents also have a person who works directly with them. This person is called either the vice-president or the deputy president. The vice-president usually is selected by the president before the election. Some countries, however, elect their vice-president separately.

The vice-president takes over some of the ceremonial duties of the president if the president is too busy. The vice-president advises the president and is the next person in line to be president should the president die in office.

In the United States, another important job of the vice-president is to work with the Senate. If there is a tie in the Senate, the vice-president casts the vote that breaks the tie. The president cannot vote to break a tie.

Presidential System of Government

1. **What are the two job titles used to describe the job of president?**

_____

_____

2. **Below are five jobs. Circle the three jobs of the vice-president.**

Attends ceremonial duties for the president

Is the next in line should the president die

Helps create laws

Vetoes bills

3. **The president of Puerto Rico has a power that is different from the traditional role of president in other countries. Explain this difference. Your answer should be one to two complete sentences.**

_____

_____

_____

4. **Do you believe this difference is in the best interest of Puerto Rico? Express your opinion in two to three sentences.**

_____

_____

_____

_____

Presidential System of Government

5. The vice-president has the power to break a tie in the Senate. The president does not have this power. Do you think the president has influence on the

_____

_____

_____

_____

6. The president has to share powers with the legislature in the presidential system. Predict what would happen if the president has total power and did not share power. What do you think would happen to the country? Your

_____

_____

_____

_____

_____

_____

_____

_____

NAME: _____

Parliamentary System of Government

1. Complete each sentence with a word from the list. Use a dictionary to help you.

execute	parliament	select
monarch	indefinite	

a) The beach is closed for an _____ period of time.

b) _____ passed a new safety law this week.

c) Only skilled riders can _____ skateboard tricks.

d) It is difficult to _____ one cake because they all look delicious.

e) The _____ waved to the crowd at the state parade.

2. Many governments follow the parliamentary system of government. List five countries that follow the parliamentary system. Use the resources in your classroom to help you.

a) _____

b) _____

c) _____

d) _____

e) _____

Parliamentary System of Government

The parliamentary system of government is a government where the ability to create and execute laws is held by the legislature. The legislature is often called a Parliament. This is the most common system of government in the world.

Countries with a parliamentary system of government do not elect their head of government. They elect their representatives in the Parliament. The members of Parliament then select the head of government. In other words, the people of the country do not decide who should be their prime minister.

Once the Parliament selects a head of government, the head of state must approve the choice. In many countries, the head of state is a monarch. In other countries, the head of state is a president. The head of state participates in ceremonies and agrees to the laws created by the representatives. They do not make laws.

There are several different names for the head of government. This depends on the country. In England, the head of government is called the prime minister. This is the most common name. In Italy, the head of the government is called the premier. In a few countries, the head of government is called a president.

Prime ministers select a cabinet just like a president in the presidential system of government. These advisors give advice to the prime minister and support the decisions made by the prime minister. The prime minister does not have to

What are the three different names used for the head of government around the world?

_____

_____

Parliamentary System of Government

follow the cabinet's advice, but they do listen to their suggestions when making decisions.

Prime ministers are chosen for an indefinite period of time. This means that the prime minister stays in power as long as the Parliament supports the prime minister. If Parliament no longer supports the prime minister, the prime minister and his cabinet are expected to step down.

Many people believe that the parliamentary system best represents all the people of a country. Members of a Parliament can represent different races, social groups, and religious groups more directly than in the presidential system.

This is because more people have more direct impact on the creation of laws and decisions than in the presidential system. Only the president has the executive power in the presidential system, but those powers are shared by a group of people in the parliamentary system.

Other people believe the parliamentary system is better because it is easier to pass laws than the presidential system. This is because the prime minister is selected by the Parliament. In the presidential system, laws that are necessary may not be approved if the president and representatives are from different political parties and do not agree.

Parliamentary System of Government

1. **Below are six statements.** (Circle) **the three statements that are true about the parliamentary system of government.**

> The head of state approves the prime minister.
>
> The prime minister creates the laws of a country.
>
> Parliament is elected by the people.
>
> Parliament chooses the prime minister.
>
> The prime minister is elected by the people.
>
> Only the prime minister has executive power.

2. **What is the role of the head of state?**

    _____

    _____

    _____

3. **In your own words, describe how a person becomes the prime minister. Your answer should be three to four sentences.**

    _____

    _____

    _____

    _____

    _____

NAME: _____

Parliamentary System of Government

4. **Explain why it is easier to pass laws in the parliamentary system than in the presidential system. Your answer should be at least three to four**

_____

_____

_____

_____

_____

5. **Do you think the people should elect their head of government or do you think the representatives elected by the people should choose their head**

_____

_____

_____

_____

_____

_____

_____

NAME: _____

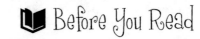 Before You Read

A Dictatorship Government

1. **Match each of the words below with the correct meaning. You may use a dictionary to help you.**

a [_____] _____ A [To set up]

b [_____] _____ B [_____]

c [_____] _____ C [_____]

d [install] _____ D [_____]

e [funding] _____ E [_____]

2. **After World War II and during the Cold War, many countries in Latin America, Africa, and Asia became dictatorship governments. Provide two reasons why this might have happened.**

   a) _____

   b) _____

3. **Identify five countries that had dictatorship governments after World War II. You may use the resources in your classroom to help you.**

   a) _____

   b) _____

   c) _____

   d) _____

   e) _____

A Dictatorship Government

A dictator is a ruler who has absolute power. A dictatorship government is ruled by a dictator. Dictatorship governments are usually the result of military rule after a war or a conflict. They usually rise to power in an emergency situation where the people are eager for a leader. Dictators are often military leaders who were active leaders during the war or conflict.

Dictatorship governments have been around for centuries. The Roman Republic had a position called Roman dictator. In times of trouble, these Roman dictators

Adolph Hitler 1889-1945

were given absolute power so that they could bring back order. However, men serving in this position had certain rules and laws that they were expected to follow.

Dictatorship governments changed over time. Dictators were no longer expected to follow the rules and laws of a government. Instead, dictators started to take complete power over a country.

After the end of World War II, many countries in Latin America, Asia, and Africa had dictatorship governments. This is because these countries had wars that ended European colonization. After fighting for their freedom, the military often installs a dictator so that one small group controlled by the military has all the power.

Why does the military install a dictator?

_____

_____

A Dictatorship Government

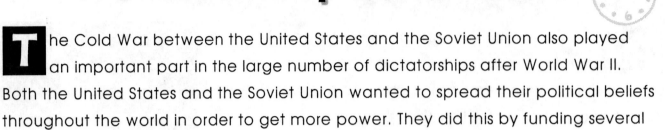

The Cold War between the United States and the Soviet Union also played an important part in the large number of dictatorships after World War II. Both the United States and the Soviet Union wanted to spread their political beliefs throughout the world in order to get more power. They did this by funding several civil wars, especially in Africa. These were brutal wars that led to the rise of a dictator.

Other countries installed dictatorships in order to protect themselves from the threat of capitalism and communism. They wanted to maintain their culture and avoid becoming just like other countries. In order to preserve their culture, they turned to a dictatorship government so that they could keep their national identity. This happened a great deal in Latin America.

In a dictatorship, the people do not have a voice in the government. The people do not have a chance to vote for their head of government. The dictator chooses all of the people who serve in the government. Countries that have dictatorship governments do not hold elections for these reasons.

Most dictatorships do not last for long periods of time. Many times, the dictator dies. Once the dictator is dead, there is often no clear way to install another dictator. The people are no longer afraid of the dictator, and they take their government back. Other times, there is another civil war, and the people take control of their government.

There are several international groups that help these countries re-establish fair and open elections. This helps them maintain control of their government.

NAME: _____

A Dictatorship Government

1. Read the five statements below. Circle the three statements that are true.

There were a large number of dictatorships after World War II.

Many dictators were former military leaders.

There are open and free elections in dictatorship governments.

Dictatorships allow the people to control their government.

2. What was the purpose of the Roman dictator?

_____

_____

3. Explain in your own words why most dictators were military leaders.

_____

_____

_____

_____

4. How has the role of a dictator changed over time? Your answer should be two to three complete sentences.

_____

_____

_____

_____

A Dictatorship Government

5. Suppose you lived in a country with a dictatorship government. Would you be satisfied with your government? Explain your answer in two to three

_____

_____

_____

_____

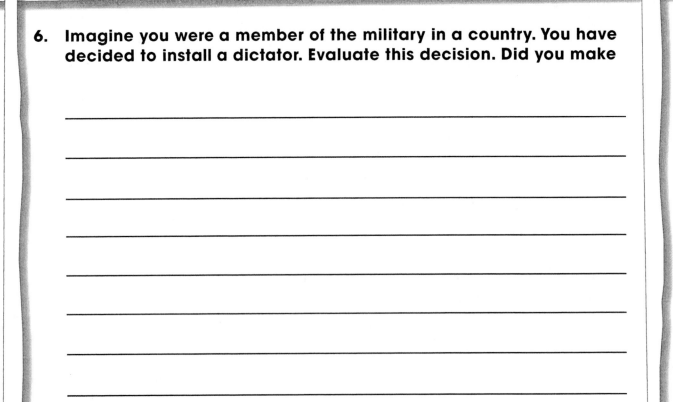

6. Imagine you were a member of the military in a country. You have decided to install a dictator. Evaluate this decision. Did you make

_____

_____

_____

_____

_____

_____

_____

Suffrage: The Voting Process, Compulsory Voting, and Voter Turnout

1. **Write each word from the list next to the correct meaning. Use a dictionary to help you.**

suffrage	compulsory	fluctuating
denied	enforce	eligible

a) Qualified _____.

b) To carry out _____.

c) The right to vote _____.

d) Turned down _____.

e) Changing _____.

f) Under command _____.

2. **Every country has its own requirements for voters. Using the resources in your classroom, find two of the requirements for voters in your country. List those requirements below.**

a) _____

_____

3. **Many countries have compulsory voting. Identify three countries. You may use the resources in your classroom to help you.**

a) _____

b) _____

c) _____

Suffrage: The Voting Process, Compulsory Voting, and Voter Turnout

Suffrage is a citizen's right to vote. In different countries throughout history, many groups have been denied suffrage. This could be because of religion, race, age, gender, or social class.

In order to vote, a citizen must meet the requirements of the country. Every country has different requirements for voting. Most countries, including Canada and the United States, require voters to be at least 18 years old. The minimum voting age throughout the world falls between 15 and 21 years old. Currently, Iran is the only country with a minimum voting age of 15.

In most countries with a democratic government, citizens have the right to decide if they are going to vote. In these countries, there are no laws that require citizens to vote. If they meet the voting requirements and are registered to vote, they are free to choose if they want to vote.

This is not the case in every country. Some countries have compulsory voting. In these countries, citizens are required by the law to vote. Other countries that have compulsory voting do not force citizens to vote, but the citizen must still come to a polling place during the election so that their name can be checked from a list.

There are laws in these countries to enforce compulsory voting. Every eligible citizen must register to vote. If people do not follow the law, they can be fined, made to complete community service hours, or even placed in jail. The consequence of breaking the law is different in each country.

Suffrage: The Voting Process, Compulsory Voting, and Voter Turnout

What are three possible consequences of breaking the law?

_____

_____

Voter turnout is very high in countries that have compulsory voting. Countries that do not have compulsory voting experience fluctuating voter turnout. One of the reasons that citizens fail to vote is that they do not register to vote. In some countries, fewer than 80% of all eligible voters register to vote.

War and media coverage can also impact voter turnout. If voters do not have confidence in their government and their leaders, they tend not to vote. Many countries are continually looking for ways to increase voter turnout, including the United States.

In many democracies, voters must register with the government in order to vote in an election. In some countries, citizens who are eligible to vote will have to fill out a form in order to register. This is the process in the United States.

Canada allows people to register to vote on their yearly income tax forms. This was intended to make the registration process easier, but it is making the process more difficult. Some people have been denied the right to vote due to mistakes. This has resulted in lowering voter turnout.

Suffrage: The Voting Process, Compulsory Voting, and Voter Turnout

1. Circle if the word **TRUE** if the statement is TRUE **or** Circle the word **FALSE** if it is FALSE.

   a) Voter turnout is not high in countries with compulsory voting.

   TRUE   **FALSE**

   b) Iran is the only country with a minimum voting age of 15.

   TRUE   **FALSE**

   c) People who do not vote in countries with compulsory voting can be put in jail.

   TRUE   **FALSE**

   d) Voting requirements are the same throughout the world.

   TRUE   **FALSE**

   e) Voters do not need to register in the United States.

   TRUE   **FALSE**

2. What is the minimum age to vote in the United States and Canada?

   _____

   _____

3. In your own words, explain how war and media coverage can impact voter turnout. Your answer should be one to two sentences.

   _____

   _____

   _____

4. Explain why voter turnout is decreasing in Canada. Your answer should be two to three sentences.

   _____

   _____

   _____

Suffrage: The Voting Process, Compulsory Voting, and Voter Turnout

5. Do you believe compulsory voting encourages people to vote or threatens them into voting? Explain your answer in two to three sentences.

_____

_____

_____

_____

6. Imagine you lived in a country with compulsory voting. Do you think you would be more or less positive about the election process? Describe how you would feel. Your answer should be

_____

_____

_____

_____

_____

_____

_____

_____

Electoral Systems and Reform

1. Complete each sentence with a word from the list. Use a dictionary to help you.

reform	ensure	fraud
component	obsolete	tampered

a) We could not finish putting the table together because we are missing one
_____.

b) I want to _____ that everyone has a cupcake before I give you
two.

c) He committed _____ when he lied about the check.

d) If you do not _____ you find yourself in serious trouble.

e) We did not purchase the aspirin because it looked like it had been
_____ with.

f) After the invention of the automobile, the horse-drawn carriage became
_____.

2. Election reforms are intended to make elections safer and more fair. Make a list of
two changes that would make elections safer and more fair.

a) _____

b) _____

3. The United Nations helps ensure safe elections. Using the resources in your classroom,
find two more facts about the United Nations.

a) _____

b) _____

Electoral Systems and Reform

Electoral systems are always changing because the needs and wants of citizens are always changing. As time goes by, countries may find that some of their electoral practices are out of date and need reform. Other countries may decide to become democracies.

A free and fair election is a major component of all democracies. If people do not have the opportunity to elect their leaders, their country is not a democracy. Whenever a country changes from a dictatorship to a democracy, there are safety concerns for the citizens.

Many times, the people who worked for the former dictator try to prevent people from voting. There are several organizations, such as the United Nations Fair Elections Commission, that can help ensure that the people can vote safely.

What does the United Nations Fair Elections Commission do?

_____

_____

Technology can also lead to electoral reform. Old voting systems may not be as accurate as new voting systems. In many countries, paper ballots that the voters punch out are becoming obsolete because they can be difficult to read. Many voting districts in the United States are changing from voting booths to computerized voting because the results are faster.

Voter fraud is a common concern for voters. There have been many elections around the world that have been effected by fraud. Voter intimidation is one way fraud can effect an election. People have even threatened violence and made bomb threats in order to disrupt elections.

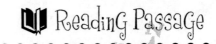

Electoral Systems and Reform

Sometimes the actual votes are tampered with in order to change the election results. Ballot stuffing occurs when one person votes more than once, causing one candidate to appear to receive more votes.

Ballot Box

Another practice is to break the election equipment, making it impossible for people to cast their vote. Or, people can tamper with voting machines so that the voting results will be in favor of one candidate, regardless of how voters actually voted.

In many places, voters have claimed to be other people in order to vote more than once. This is becoming more difficult in most countries because voters have to show identification before they vote. However, there are countries where people do not have identification, and this type of voter fraud is easier.

Voting machines have even been tampered with in order to change the results of an election. This can be done many different ways, including tampering with the voting machine software. As computer software becomes more complex, it becomes harder to tamper with election results.

Election systems are always changing in order to best serve the voters. Reform is a necessary part of the electoral process because it is designed to make sure elections are fair. True democracies are always looking for better ways to improve their electoral systems.

Electoral Systems and Reform

1. Below is a list of five statements. Circle the three statements that are true about electoral reform.

> Ballot stuffing is a fair electoral process.
>
> Reform helps make elections fair.
>
> Technology can lead to election reform.
>
> Voting machines cannot be tampered with.
>
> Electoral systems are always changing.

2. What is voter fraud?

_____

_____

3. In your own words, explain how ballot stuffing can impact an election. Your answer should be two to three complete sentences.

_____

_____

_____

4. Why are democracies always working toward electoral reform? Your answer should be one to two complete sentences.

_____

_____

_____

Electoral Systems and Reform

5. Predict what would happen if it was discovered your president or prime minister tampered with the election. Your answer should be at least three to four sentences.

_____

_____

_____

_____

_____

6. In your opinion, what should be the consequences of tampering with an election?

_____

_____

_____

_____

_____

_____

_____

Writing Tasks

1. Imagine that you could be the next leader of your country. What issues would be important to your voters. Write a speech, describing what you would do if you were given the power to lead your country.

2. Is your country's government a dictatorship, or does it follow either the presidential or parliamentary system of government? Use specific examples from the text you have read to support your answer.

3. Which form of government do you think best represents the citizens? Provide three examples that substantiate your opinion.

4. Complete the "Dictator vs. Elected Leader" graphic organizer. In your essay, compare and contrast the two different types of leadership. Be sure to give examples from your reading and research in order to support your answer.

5. Voter turnout is becoming a very large problem in the electoral process. What can be done to improve voter turnout? Create a plan that would help improve voter turnout in your area. Suggest three ideas to improve voter turnout and describe how these ideas can become reality.

6. Select a prime minister, president, or dictator from the 20th century. Complete the "Biography Timeline" graphic organizer. Write a biography of this leader, including how the leader came into power and how their leadership was impacted by world events.

Hands-on Activities

1. **Basketball Review Game:** At the end of the unit, you can use this game to help you prepare students for a unit quiz or test. Affix a basketball hoop to a wall in your classroom. On the floor in front of the basket, adhere three lines to the floor using tape. Assign each of these lines a point value. The closest line to the basket should be one point, the middle line should be two points, and the farthest line should be three points. Students will be divided into two teams, and one player will be at the hoop at a time. When the player answers the question correctly, they will throw a soft ball at the hoop in order to get points. If they miss the hoop or do not answer the question correctly, they will not be awarded points.

   Before starting the activity, you will need to prepare three categories of questions: easy (1 point), medium (2 points), and challenging (3 points). You can even involve the students in writing the questions. The day before the basketball game, ask each student to write one of each type of question. You can then go through those questions and select the best questions for the game.

2. **Hold an Election:** Select a policy or rule that would be relevant to the running of your classroom. This could include how chores are divided or whether or not homework will be assigned on weekends for one month. Students will have to work together to decide when the election will be held, design a ballot for the election, create a voting system that allows for voting privacy and security, and decide how votes will be counted.

3. **Roleplay:** In the paliamentary system, the House of Representatives allows members to deliver 90 second statements about issues that are important to them. Allow students to select their own issues and speak as a member of Parliament for those 90 seconds. Each student should have the opportunity to roleplay, so you will need to set aside ample time. You may decide to act as the Speaker, the moderator of the statements, or you may decide to select a student to be the moderator. If you do decide to allow a student to be the Speaker, make sure that student can keep track of the time limitations before you begin the statements.

Dictator vs. Elected Leader Graphic Organizer

Directions: In the two outer columns, list the characteristics of each type of leadership. In the inner column, list the characteristics that are similar.

DICTATOR	SIMILARITIES	ELECTED LEADER

Biography Timeline
Graphic Organizer

Directions: Use the timeline below to organize your biography project. In the empty boxes, write major events in the order they happened in that leader's life on the right side. On the left side, write the date of the events.

NAME: _____

Crossword Puzzle!

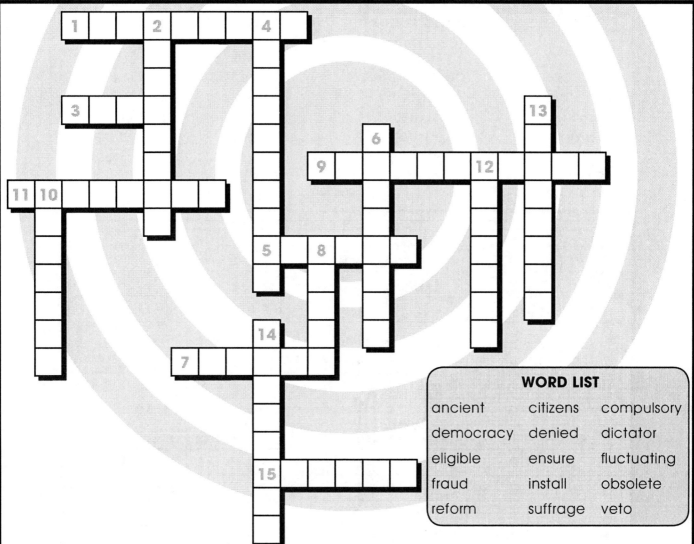

WORD LIST

ancient	citizens	compulsory
democracy	denied	dictator
eligible	ensure	fluctuating
fraud	install	obsolete
reform	suffrage	veto

Across

1. A government by the people
3. The power of a president to stop a law
5. To change
7. Turned down
9. Changing
11. A leader with absolute power
15. To make certain

Down

2. Out of date
4. Under command
6. The right to vote
8. Trickery
10. To set up
12. Very old
13. Qualified
14. The people of a country

NAME: _____

 After You Read

Word Search

Find all of the words in the Word Search. Words are written horizontally, vertically, diagonally, and some are even written backwards.

option	select	obsolete	bill
monarch	component	democracy	suffrage
fluctuating	election	install	veto
cast	dictator	fraud	denied
parliament	ensure	term	cabinet
reform	citizens	funding	enforce
medieval	military	execute	

T	C	E	L	E	S	R	S	E	T	U	C	E	X	E	G	H	F
U	W	E	O	L	T	K	O	B	S	O	L	E	T	E	N	J	L
F	Y	T	P	U	O	T	D	I	N	E	T	E	T	P	T	Z	U
H	O	P	T	I	O	N	O	I	T	C	E	L	E	N	A	C	C
M	T	E	S	U	F	F	R	A	G	E	N	T	R	F	M	U	T
Q	A	W	A	N	H	E	S	R	H	T	I	P	M	J	P	L	U
U	E	F	C	K	C	A	B	I	N	E	T	R	R	T	E	G	A
V	D	E	R	U	S	N	E	S	R	H	O	E	R	O	R	E	T
F	E	R	T	H	Y	V	S	E	K	T	W	F	O	Y	E	L	I
I	X	T	C	Y	F	L	L	U	A	B	J	O	T	U	D	E	N
N	W	E	O	A	S	A	U	T	T	O	J	R	K	F	J	E	G
S	E	F	A	M	V	N	C	D	V	H	I	M	A	D	Q	D	S
T	O	E	C	E	S	I	Q	A	C	E	R	C	U	V	A	C	X
A	S	W	I	C	D	E	U	R	V	O	M	A	T	K	P	O	O
L	T	D	T	J	K	D	A	C	R	Y	R	L	U	D	Z	M	A
L	E	N	I	A	B	N	S	H	U	F	C	T	W	E	N	P	P
M	E	R	Z	F	O	T	A	P	T	H	J	C	A	N	P	O	G
P	S	D	E	M	O	C	R	A	C	Y	R	E	N	I	T	N	L
O	I	R	N	E	Y	E	N	F	O	R	C	E	G	E	I	E	U
I	A	W	S	N	P	R	J	W	S	E	T	S	K	D	B	N	L
R	M	I	L	I	T	A	R	Y	G	S	I	Q	N	P	R	T	E
A	Q	L	U	T	K	E	T	A	K	H	R	U	O	L	U	T	J

World Politics – Big Book CC5777

NAME: _____

Comprehension Quiz

Part A

25

Circle if the word **TRUE** if the statement is TRUE **or** Circle the word **FALSE** if it is FALSE.

5

a) The people elect the prime minister.

TRUE   FALSE

b) Technology can lead to electoral reform.

TRUE   FALSE

c) There are free and open elections in a dictatorship.

TRUE   FALSE

d) The ancient Romans were the first to vote.

TRUE   FALSE

e) Women have not always been allowed to vote

TRUE   FALSE

Part B

Match the term on the left with the correct definition on the right.

5

1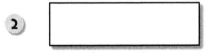

A The power to stop a law

2

B

3

C

4

D

5

E

SUBTOTAL: /10

Comprehension Quiz

Part C

Answer the questions in complete sentences.

1. Explain the purpose of the cabinet.

_____

_____

_____

(3)

2. Explain how technology can cause electoral reform.

_____

_____

_____

(3)

3. How long is a prime minister's term of office?

_____

_____

_____

(3)

4. Identify two reasons why people have been denied the right to vote.

_____

_____

_____

(3)

5. How does compulsory voting affect voter turnout?

_____

_____

_____

(3)

SUBTOTAL: /15

 Before You Read

The Rise of Capitalism in the Late 19th Century and Following the Great Depression

1. Match each of the words below with the correct meaning. You may use a dictionary to help you.

1	economy	Large businesses	A
2	monopoly	The management of money	B
3	stock	Out of money	C
4	corporations	An industry controlled by one person or group	D
5	bankrupt	Shares of a company	E

2. During the Great Depression, millions of Americans were unemployed. Imagine if your country experienced a similar depression. **List fives ways** your country would change.

a) _____

b) _____

c) _____

d) _____

e) _____

3. President Franklin Delano Roosevelt created the New Deal to help his country recover. Use the resources in your classroom to **find three facts** about the New Deal. List those facts below.

a) _____

b) _____

c) _____

Reading Passage

NAME: _____

The Rise of Capitalism in the Late 19th Century and Following the Great Depression

Capitalism is an economic system where businesses can be owned by private citizens. Many people believe that when people own their business, there is more competition because people will be more interested in making more money.

Capitalism is one of the oldest economic systems in the world. During the late 19th century, many changes occurred in business that changed capitalism forever. The first change was the creation of large monopolies. Before this time, businesses were small, but technology and other changes allowed companies to grow bigger.

Another change was that the people who owned and managed the businesses were no longer involved in the daily production of the companies. In fact, some owners never set foot in the companies they managed.

Because companies wanted to get bigger, they started selling company stock in order to have more cash on hand. Regular people started buying this stock, and banking became more developed as a result. In fact, buying stock became a very popular habit because people had more money to spend than they had in the past.

STOP

Why do companies sell their stock?

_____

_____

_____

NAME: _____

The Rise of Capitalism in the Late 19th Century and Following the Great Depression

Corporations grew into very large companies that were very powerful. The U.S. government created laws to protect people from monopolies, but many of these laws only helped large companies get more power.

Cycles of economic depressions and prosperity became a problem. The economy would be very strong, and then the economy would crash down without warning. The economy became very unpredictable. As a result, people began to doubt that Capitalism could really work.

The most difficult time in the history of Capitalism was the time following the Great Depression. In 1929, the U.S. stock market crashed. Thousands of people in the United States became bankrupt because they had invested their money in stock.

Businesses also suffered and many went out of business. This meant that the workers lost their jobs, and there were not enough jobs for everyone who needed to work. Between 1932 and 1933, over 16 million Americans were unemployed. This was one third of the U.S. work force.

Businesses in Europe were also impacted by the Great Depression. These countries were still trying to recover from World War I before the Great Depression. As a result of the Depression, these countries suffered. It is believed that Germany's struggle after World War I and the Depression led to Adolf Hitler's rise to power.

President Franklin Delano Roosevelt created many new programs to help the U.S. recover from the Depression. This was called the New Deal. The programs created in the New Deal created jobs for the unemployed and helped the country recover.

Recovery from the Great Depression took a very long time. Experts say that businesses did not fully recover from the Depression until the 1940's.

The Rise of Capitalism in the Late 19th Century and Following the Great Depression

1. During the late 19th century, many changes occurred in business. (Circle) the four changes that occurred.

   a) Small businesses became more popular.

   b) Banking became more developed.

   c) Large monopolies were created.

   d) Owners and managers were not involved in daily production.

   e) Large companies stopped selling stock.

   f) People started purchasing stock in companies.

2. Explain the impact of competition on business.

   _____

   _____

   _____

   _____

   _____

3. The United States created laws to protect people from monopolies. Explain why these laws did not work.

   _____

   _____

   _____

   _____

   _____

The Rise of Capitalism in the Late 19th Century and Following the Great Depression

4. The New Deal was created as a result of the Great Depression. Explain how the New Deal helped the United States recover. Your answer should be two to three complete sentences.

_____

_____

_____

_____

5. Explain the connection between the Great Depression in the United States and the rise of Adolf Hitler in Germany. How are the two events linked? Your answer should be two to three complete sentences.

_____

_____

_____

_____

6. Imagine you were the U.S. president at the time of the Great Depression. What steps would you have taken to help the country recover? Your answer should be three to four complete sentences.

_____

_____

_____

_____

NAME: _____

The Industrial Revolution

1. Write each word from the list next to the correct meaning. Use a dictionary to help you.

significant	consumer	transport
manual	goods	initially

[ ]	**a)** Worked or created by hand
[ ]	**b)** At first
[ ]	**c)** Major
[ ]	**d)** A person that buys goods
[ ]	**e)** Something for sale
[ ]	**f)** To move from one place to another

2. As a result of the Industrial Revolution, many inventions were created. Use the resources in your classroom to list four of those inventions.

a) _____

b) _____

c) _____

d) _____

3. Imagine what your life would be like without factories. Make a list of five items you would not have in your everyday life if there were no factories.

a) _____

b) _____

c) _____

d) _____

The Industrial Revolution

T he Industrial Revolution began in England during the mid 18th century. The Revolution spread quickly throughout the world.

There was a significant change during the Industrial Revolution. Before the Industrial Revolution, most labor was manual labor. This included farm work. After the Revolution, manual labor was replaced by machine work in factories.

As a result, more factories were created. More and more people started working in factories. Cities began to grow bigger and bigger as more people moved to work in the factories.

During the Industrial Revolution, many machines were invented so that factories could be more productive. Consumer demand was high because people had more money to spend on goods. Machinery made it much easier to make those goods quickly, so prices dropped. This allowed people to purchase even more goods.

At this time, the steam engine was invented. The steam engine was initially used in mining, but it was later used to help power the machines in large factories.

STOP

What was the steam engine initially used for?

_____

_____

_____

NAME: _____

The Industrial Revolution

Transporting goods also became much easier during the Industrial Revolution. Canals and roads were improved in order to help make delivering goods easier and faster. The railroad system developed quickly, especially after the development of the steam engine. This made transporting goods across large countries very fast and safe.

The population increased as a result of the Industrial Revolution. There was more food and more money, so more healthy children were born than ever before. More children survived childhood because they were able to eat regular, healthy meals. People began to live longer lives.

There were more children, but children were expected to help their families. There were not many educational programs for children, and poor families needed the money their children earned to survive. Children were expected to work in the factories and other dangerous conditions. Many children died while working in these factories.

Many people were openly critical about child labor. They were also critical of other changes as a result of the Industrial Revolution. They felt that companies were getting too large.

They also worried that a few people were getting very rich while a large number of people stayed poor. They became interested in a system that is very different from Capitalism. That system is Communism.

NAME: _____

The Industrial Revolution

1. **Circle** the word **TRUE** if the statement is TRUE **or** **Circle** the word **FALSE** if it is FALSE.

   a) The steam engine was invented before the Industrial Revolution.

         TRUE   **FALSE**

   b) The Industrial Revolution started in North America.

         TRUE   **FALSE**

   c) Educational programs for children were not available to everyone.

         TRUE   **FALSE**

   d) Railroads became important in transporting goods.

         TRUE   **FALSE**

   e) Farming became very popular in the Industrial Revolution.

         TRUE   **FALSE**

2. **When did the Industrial Revolution begin?**

   _____

   _____

   _____

3. Compare labor before the Industrial Revolution to labor during the Industrial Revolution. How did labor change? Your answer should be two to three sentences.

   _____

   _____

   _____

   _____

After You Read

NAME: _____

The Industrial Revolution

4. What impact did the Industrial Revolution have on cities? Your answer should be two to three sentences.

_____

_____

_____

_____

_____

5. Explain why people became more interested in Communism as a result of the changes caused by the Industrial Revolution. Your answer should be two to three sentences.

_____

_____

_____

_____

_____

6. Imagine you could interview a child growing up during the Industrial Revolution. List four questions you would ask that child about their life and experiences.

a) _____

b) _____

c) _____

d) _____

NAME: _____

Capitalism Since the Cold War

1. Complete each sentence with a word from the list. Use a dictionary to help you.

conflict	dissolve
method	exception

a) Sugar will [_____] in water.

b) After the [_____], the two friends stopped speaking for a while.

c) There is no [_____] to the rule in this case.

d) The [_____] used to solve the math problem is not very difficult.

2. The Cold War was a very challenging time for the entire world. Use the resources in your classroom to find four facts about the Cold War. Be prepared to share those facts with your class.

a) _____

b) _____

c) _____

d) _____

Reading Passage

NAME: _____

Capitalism Since the Cold War

T he Cold War was a troubling time for the entire world. During this time, countries with Capitalist economies were in direct conflict with countries that had Communist economies.

There were two major groups who were in conflict during the Cold War. The United Kingdom, the United States, and Western Europe were on the side of Capitalism. The Soviet Union, China, and Eastern Europe were on the side of Communism.

All of these countries wanted their economy to become the world economy. They used many methods to influence other countries to adopt their economy.

Some of these methods had negative impacts on the other countries, including the creation of dictatorship governments. This has had a lasting impact on the rest of the world.

What was the conflict that caused the Cold War?

_____

_____

When the Cold War ended, the Soviet Union began to dissolve. They began to change from a Communist economy into a Capitalist economy. This was a very difficult change that continues to challenge Russia.

The Soviet Union was divided into several smaller, independent countries. What is left of the original Soviet Union is now called Russia.

With the exception of the People's Republic of China, all major countries in the world now have Capitalist economies of some form. Other countries that have Communist economies are Laos, Cuba, North Korea, and Vietnam.

However, Capitalism has changed since the Cold War. Business has become more global than ever. Both goods and ideas are being shared freely throughout most of the world.

NAME: _____

Capitalism Since the Cold War

1. **Below are six countries. Categorize the countries according to their beliefs.**

Eastern Europe	**Cuba**	**Western Europe**
The United States	**The United Kingdom**	**The Soviet Union**

Communism

_____

_____

_____

Capitalism

_____

_____

_____

2. Explain why Capitalist countries and Communist countries were engaged in a conflict with each other.

_____

_____

_____

3. Describe how the end of the Cold War impacted the Soviet Union. Your answer should be at least two to three sentences.

_____

_____

_____

4. The world is becoming more globalized. Do you think this is a positive change or a negative change? Be sure to provide examples that support your opinion. Your answer should be three to four sentences.

_____

_____

_____

Freedom of the Market & Individuals

1. Complete each sentence with a word from the list. Use a dictionary to help you.

foundation	supply	option
regulate	demand	

a) We had to take the floor model because there was no other [ ].

b) There is a high [ ] for nurses because of the shortage.

c) The [ ] of the house is crumbling and needs to be repaired.

d) It is not the job of the government to [ ] prices in a free market economy.

e) We have a large [ ] of canned goods in the basement should a large snowstorm arise.

2. Make a list of two items that you purchase on a regular basis. These items should be things you use on a daily basis.

a) _____

b) _____

3. Imagine there is only one store in your area and it only has a few of each item in the store. Do you think the price would be higher or lower than usual? Explain your answer in one to two sentences.

_____

_____

_____

NAME: _____

Freedom of the Market & Individuals

Freedom is an important right that is not protected in all types of governments. In a democracy, citizens enjoy many freedoms. The ability to choose from many different options is the foundation of democracy.

A free market economy is a part of democracy. In a free market, the price for an item is not regulated by the government. Instead, the price for an item is determined by buyers and sellers through supply and demand.

STOP

How are prices determined in a free market economy?

_____

_____

The law of supply and demand helps determine the price people will pay for an item. If the supply of an item is high but very few people want the item, the price will be low. If many people want an item that is in low supply, the price will be high.

Communist governments do not allow free market economies. In governments that do not have free markets, there are very few options available to the citizens. They do not have the freedom to go to a store, look at several items, and choose one that they like.

Shopping is very different in Communist countries. There may be only one or two stores. Prices will often be higher because they are regulated by the government. People do not shop as a recreational activity as they do in many Capitalistic countries.

Individuals do not have the freedom to shop around for the best deal in a Communist country. They also are limited by the number of choices that are available to them.

In fact, there may be only one of a particular item in a store. The supply of goods in Communist countries is usually low, but the demand is great. Prices are set by the government, but they are also usually high.

Without a free market economy, citizens do not have the freedom to make everyday decisions. They are limited by the decisions of their government.

After You Read 📖

NAME: _____

Freedom of the Market & Individuals

1. Circle the word **TRUE** if the statement is TRUE **or** Circle the word **FALSE** if it is FALSE.

   a) Communist governments have free market economies.

   TRUE   **FALSE**

   b) Prices are set by the government in free market economies.

   TRUE   **FALSE**

   c) There are very few choices in Communist countries.

   TRUE   **FALSE**

   d) It is easy to shop for the best deal in Communist countries.

   TRUE   **FALSE**

2. In your own words, explain the law of supply and demand. Your answer should be two to three complete sentences.

   _____

   _____

   _____

Freedom of the Market & Individuals

3. People in Communist countries cannot go to the mall and buy the items they need. There are fewer goods available to people, and they do not have many options when goods are available for purchase. You have the opportunity to interview a person from a Communist country. List four questions you would ask them about shopping in their country.

a) _____

b) _____

c) _____

d) _____

4. Which type of market do you think is best? Explain your answer in three to four complete sentences.

_____

_____

_____

_____

5. What changes would you make to help make Communist markets more free. Make three suggestions that would help improve the market. Your answer should be three to four sentences.

_____

_____

_____

_____

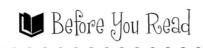

NAME: _____

A Capitalistic Political Economy

1. **Match each of the words below with the correct meaning. You may use a dictionary to help you.**

1	operate		The act of interfering	A
2	enterprise		Not legal or moral	B
3	intervention		To cause to work	C
4	merchant		A business organization	D
5	corrupt		Someone who sells items at a profit	E

2. Earlier, you learned about the Industrial Revolution. List four facts about the Industrial Revolution below.

a) _____

b) _____

c) _____

d) _____

3. Using the resources in your classroom, list three countries that have Capitalistic political economies.

a) _____

b) _____

c) _____

NAME: _____

A Capitalistic Political Economy

A country that allows private citizens to own and operate their own businesses has a Capitalistic political economy. In this system, individuals are allowed the freedom to own their own businesses in order to make money.

The foundation of Capitalism is the idea of free enterprise. This means the individual control their business. The individual has the right to create their own business, decide what they want to produce, and make money. Individuals also have the right to purchase whatever goods they desire.

The government cannot control the economy or tell people what to buy, make, or sell. All of these decisions are made by the people who own the businesses and purchase the goods produced by the businesses.

Prices are not regulated by the government in a Capitalist economy. Capitalist countries have a free market economy. Prices are determined by the law of supply and demand. It is believed that this protects the freedom and interests of the people.

Some experts believe that Capitalism has existed in some form since the invention of agriculture. Farmers chose their own crops and sold their crops at a price that was fair. This is a very basic form of Capitalism.

NAME: _____

A Capitalistic Political Economy

Capitalism became an important political economy during the Industrial Revolution. During this time, factory owners, bankers, and merchants began to become very powerful. This caused more businesses to become privately owned by private citizens.

STOP

When did Capitalism become an important political economy?

_____

_____

Many critics of Capitalism say that government intervention is necessary in order to protect the people. They believe that the foundation of Capitalism, the free market, can easily become corrupt. They believe that it is very easy for one person or group to gain too much power. That is why they believe that the government should control the market.

Corruption is a risk in a Capitalistic political economy. If the government and the people are not careful in a Capitalistic political economy, monopolies can develop. This happens when a person or a company controls a market or an industry. This can lead to corruption, which can cause the prices of goods to rise significantly.

Governments do carefully monitor both businesses and industries in order to protect the people from a monopoly. A government can create laws and regulations to prevent the creation of a monopoly. This is one way a Capitalist government can protect their rights and interests of its citizens.

A Capitalistic Political Economy

1. Below are five statements. (Circle) the three ideas that are a part of a Capitalistic political economy.

    a) Individuals can own their own businesses.

    b) Supply and demand determines the prices.

    c) The government can tell factories what they can produce.

    d) It is not possible for a Capitalistic political economy to become corrupt.

    e) Governments can create laws to prevent the development of monopolies.

2. In your own words, create a definition for the idea of free enterprise. Your definition should be one to two sentences.

_____

_____

3. How did Capitalism change during the Industrial Revolution? Your answer should be two to three complete sentences.

_____

_____

_____

4. Explain why monopolies are dangerous to the citizens. Your answer should be two to three complete sentences.

_____

_____

_____

5. Imagine that you are a government representative in a Capitalistic country. What steps would you take to protect your citizens from the development of monopolies? Your plan should be three to four complete sentences.

_____

_____

_____

NAME: _____

A Communist Political Economy

1. Write each word from the list next to the correct meaning. Use a dictionary to help you.

permitted	emerged	decade
fragmented	nations	

☐   **a)** Countries

☐   **b)** A period of ten years

☐   **c)** Allowed

☐   **d)** Broken into pieces

☐   **e)** Came into being

2. During the Cold War, Communism spread very quickly in Eastern Europe, Asia, and in Africa. Use the resources in your classroom to list three facts about the Cold War to share with your class.

a) _____

b) _____

c) _____

3. Use the resources in your classroom to identify three countries that have Communist political economies.

a) _____

b) _____

c) _____

NAME: _____

A Communist Political Economy

Communism is a political economy where property is shared by the people equally. This means that individuals are not permitted to own private businesses. Instead, businesses are owned and operated by the government.

Communism has been in existence for many centuries. Many Native American cultures had systems that were similar to Communism. For example, the Incas worked together to grow food. This food was then shared equally by the community. No one community member profited more than any other community member.

The Industrial Revolution also had an effect on the development of Communism. One of the problems that emerged from the Industrial Revolution was a growing number of poor factory workers. These workers recognized that their hard work made factory owners rich, not them. People began to become interested in a system that would allow the profit to be shared equally by all the workers.

In 1917, the Russian Revolution was won by the Bolsheviks who believed in the Communist system. They then created the Communist party and formed the Soviet Union. The Communist party led the Soviet Union for decades.

STOP

Who won the Russian Revolution?

_____

_____

A Communist Political Economy

The entire world became more fragmented as a result of World Wars I and II. Both Communist countries and Capitalist countries wanted other countries to use their system so that they could become more powerful. Many countries that suffered after both wars decided to become Communist countries. Communism spread quickly in Eastern Europe and Asia.

Other countries became Communist countries as a result of a civil war. In fact, many of these wars were paid for by both Communist and Capitalist countries so that they could have more power in the area. As a result, Communism also spread quickly in some nations in the Middle East, Africa, and Central America.

Many people who are critical of Communism believe that this system can be easily corrupted by the government. They believe the government has too much power and does not equally share all the resources with the citizens.

When the Cold War ended, many countries abandoned Communism. By 1990, Poland, East Germany, Hungary, and other Eastern European nations all abandoned Communism and adopted more Capitalistic economic systems. In 1991, the Soviet Union dissolved and changed its name back to Russia.

There are still several countries in the world that follow the Communist system. They are primarily in Asia, but can be found elsewhere in the world.

A Communist Political Economy

1. Below are pairs of events. (**Circle**) **the event that happened first in each pair of events.**

a) The Bolsheviks won the Russian Revolution.

The Communist party led the Soviet Union for decades.

b) The Industrial Revolution occurred.

The Cold War began.

c) East Germany abandoned Communism.

The Soviet Union dissolved

2. Below are four statements. Draw a box around the two statements that are true about Communism.

Individuals cannot own or operate their own businesses.

The government cannot tell people what to buy, make, or sell.

Business owners make all the profit.

Everyone receives an equal share of the profit.

3. Explain how the Inca culture was similar to Communism. Your answer should be two to three complete sentences.

_____

_____

_____

_____

_____

_____

A Communist Political Economy

4. How did the Industrial Revolution help the development of Communism? Your answer should be two to three sentences.

_____

_____

_____

_____

_____

5. How did the Cold War impact Communism? Your answer should be two to three sentences.

_____

_____

_____

_____

_____

6. Do you believe that a Communist system could actually work and not be corrupted? In your opinion, give a specific example to support your opinion. Your answer should be four to five sentences.

_____

_____

_____

_____

_____

NAME: _____

A Globalization Economy

1. Complete each sentence with a word from the list. Use a dictionary to help you.

constantly	interact
exposed	globalize

a) We were _____ to the flu virus at the hospital.

b) Once we _____ production, we will be able to sell our products everywhere.

c) The movie was _____ interrupted by ringing cell phones.

d) At the party, we will have to _____ with people we have never met before.

2. Make a list of four items you own that were made in another country.

a) _____

b) _____

c) _____

d) _____

A Globalization Economy

The world is constantly changing as technology becomes more advanced. Computers have made the world a much different place than it was twenty years ago. One of the most recent changes that has had an impact on the world is Globalization.

Technology has allowed business to change dramatically. Businesses can now sell their products and services to a much wider market. Instead of being limited to a smaller local market, businesses can now sell their goods and services to the entire world. This means that they can reach more people, sell more products, and make more money.

Globalization allows businesses to form world-wide partnerships. This helps smaller businesses become exposed to the world-wide marketplace through their partners. In the past, small businesses throughout the world would never have had the opportunity to partner with a larger company from a different country.

Large businesses also benefit from Globalization. These companies can now find the cheapest prices for raw materials, technology, and workers. As a result, it often becomes less expensive to produce the same product. This partnership saves the larger company a great deal of money.

NAME: _____

A Globalization Economy

Globalization has had a direct impact on the economy of the United States. Before Globalization, the United States held a large percentage of the world market. After the beginning of Globalization, the United States now has 25% of the world market. Some critics fear this percentage may drop even lower and forever change American business.

After the beginning of Globalization, what happened to the United States' share of the world market?

_____

_____

Critics also say that Globalization takes jobs away from the United States. In fact, many factory jobs and software jobs have been moved to other countries. This is because businesses have found that they can produce the same goods and products at a cheaper price in another country.

Other critics support Globalization. They claim the new global economy creates the need for other countries to interact with each other. For example, a company in England may need materials from China in order to make their product. If England and China begin to have a conflict, steps will need to be taken in order to protect the economies of both countries.

Other countries will now have to depend on each other, so world leaders will have to find new ways to get along. This will help countries develop new relationships and will lead to countries learning how to settle conflict differently.

After You Read 📖

NAME: _____

A Globalization Economy

1. **Circle** the word **TRUE** if the statement is TRUE **or** **Circle** the word **FALSE** if it is FALSE.

   a) Computers have not changed the way the world does business.

      TRUE   FALSE

   b) The United States' share of the world market has increased.

      TRUE   FALSE

   c) It is now easier to get goods from around the world.

      TRUE   FALSE

   d) Only small businesses benefit from Globalization.

      TRUE   FALSE

   e) Both large and small businesses can benefit from Globalization.

      TRUE   FALSE

2. How have small businesses benefited from world-wide partnerships? Your answer should be two to three sentences.

   _____

   _____

   _____

   _____

   _____

   _____

A Globalization Economy

3. How have large businesses benefited from world-wide partnerships? Your answer should be two to three sentences.

_____

_____

_____

_____

4. What impact has Globalization had on the United States? Your answer should be three to four sentences.

_____

_____

_____

_____

5. Because of Globalization, there has been a greater need for transportation. This has had a negative impact on the environment. Develop a plan that would support Globalization and help protect the environment. Your answer should be three to four sentences.

_____

_____

_____

_____

NAME: _____

Communism in the 21st Century

1. Write each word from the list next to the correct meaning. Use a dictionary to help you.

collapse	distant	gradual	strict

	a) Slowly, over time
	b) Far away
	c) Fall apart
	d) Controlled

2. Below is a map of Asia. On the map, identify the Communist countries in Asia. You can use the resources in your classroom to help you.

a) Color China blue
b) Color North Korea red.
c) Color Laos green.
d) Color Vietnam orange.

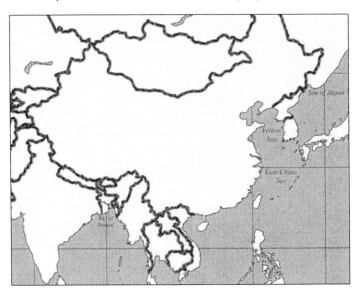

3. How far away is Cuba from the United States? Use the resources in your classroom to help you.

_____

_____

NAME: _____

Communism in the 21st Century

There are significantly fewer Communist countries in the world since the collapse of the Soviet Union. The only Communist countries in the world are China, Cuba, Vietnam, North Korea, and Laos.

The most influential Communist country is China. China is a major world power and has the world's highest population. In the late 20th century, China has made several changes that are Capitalistic changes. Citizens are now allowed to own private businesses. Experts believe that this is a step towards a gradual change to Capitalism.

Cuba is the closest Communist country to the United States. However, the United States has a very distant relationship with Cuba. U.S. citizens are not allowed to travel to Cuba, and the United States will not trade with Cuba. As a result, life in Cuba has been very difficult for the citizens of Cuba. Many Cubans have moved to the U.S. because life in Cuba has become too difficult.

 **Why have many Cubans come to live in the United States?**

_____

_____

Cuba has had only one leader the entire time it has been a Communist country. This leader is Fidel Castro, who helped lead the Cuban Revolution. He has been in power for several decades. It is believed by many experts that when Castro dies, Cuba will become a Capitalist country.

North Korea is a very strict Communist country. The government closely controls the economy and most of the components of social and academic life. In North Korea, it is against the law to express opinions that are not in agreement with the government. It is also against the law to study certain subjects and read certain books because they disagree with the North Korean government.

Several other countries also have active Communist parties, but the countries are not Communist countries. These countries include Italy, India, the United States, and many other countries.

Communism in the 21st Century

1. Identify the five Communist countries discussed in the reading.

a) _____

b) _____

c) _____

d) _____

e) _____

2. What change has China recently made that makes the country more Capitalistic?

_____

_____

_____

_____

3. What impact has the United States' position on Communism had on the country of Cuba? Your answer should be two to three sentences.

_____

_____

_____

_____

_____

Communism in the 21st Century

4. Describe what you imagine life in North Korea to be like. Your answer should be at least three to four sentences.

_____

_____

_____

_____

5. What do you believe will happen to Communism in the future? Provide examples to support your opinion. Your answer should be three to four complete sentences.

_____

_____

_____

_____

6. You have the opportunity to interview a person who strongly believes in the future of Communism. List four questions you would ask this individual.

a) _____

b) _____

c) _____

d) _____

Writing Tasks

1. Select one of the inventions that were created during the Industrial Revolution. Write a one page report that includes the inventor, a description of the invention, and how the invention changed business.

2. The Great Depression was a challenging time for people in the United States and throughout the world. Imagine you are growing up during this time. Write a one page diary entry from the perspective of a person living during the Great Depression.

3. Consider the new Globalization economy. How will the world change as a result of Globalization? In your essay, describe three changes. Provide specific examples to help support your prediction. Use the Globalization Economy Organizer to help you.

4. How has Communism changed after the fall of the Soviet Union? List three examples and provide details to support your answer.

5. Communist governments tend not to last as long as Capitalist governments. Explain several reasons why this trend is true.

6. Compare Communism to Capitalism. Use the Communism vs. Capitalism Organizer to help you plan your essay.

Globalization Economy Organizer

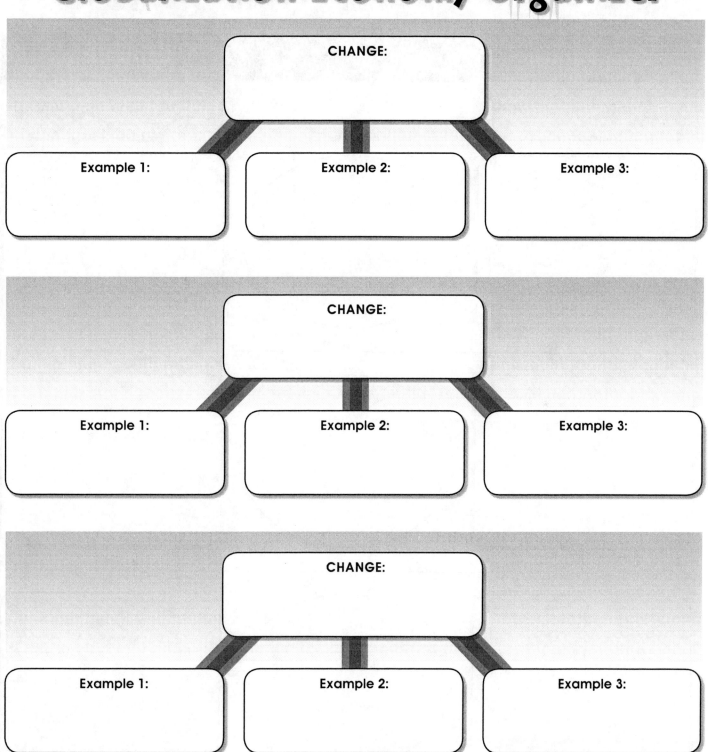

CHANGE:

Example 1:

Example 2:

Example 3:

CHANGE:

Example 1:

Example 2:

Example 3:

CHANGE:

Example 1:

Example 2:

Example 3:

Hands-On Activity #3

Communism vs. Capitalism Organizer

Communism		Capitalism
DIFFERENT	**SAME**	**DIFFERENT**

World Politics – Big Book CC5777

1. **Grocery Shopping:** Divide the class into two separate groups: shoppers and shop keepers. Ask the shoppers to make a list of everything they would need in order to make their lunch, including bread, meat, and fruits/vegetables. Once you have approved their lists, you can then send the shoppers to the store owners.

Store keepers will be provided with a stack of numbered paper slips. They will be instructed to hand these numbers to the shoppers after the shoppers have read their lists to the shop keepers. Shoppers will then have to wait until their number is called. Once their number is called, some will receive partial food orders, while others will be told that they will have to come back at a later date.

After this activity, you can discuss how this shopping experience differs from the everyday shopping experience in the Western world. What are the pros and cons of each system? You can create a list as a class and display it in your classroom.

2. **Globalization Map:** Provide each student with a desk-sized map of the United States, Mexico, and Asia. Each student should also have twenty coins. In the beginning, all twenty coins should be placed on the United States. You will then read the following statements to the students, and they will move their coins as instructed.

1. The Rebound shoe company uses materials and constructs their shoes in American factories. Keep all twenty coins in America.

2. It is discovered that plastic soles are cheaper when they are made in Korea. Take five coins from the United States and place them on Korea.

3. A new study shows that material made in Mexico can save millions a year. Move seven coins from the United States to Mexico.

4. Count the coins left in the United States. Eight coins should be left.

You can then lead a class discussion on the impact of globalization on the United States. You can even work in conjunction with the Math teacher in order to run statistics and create graphs.

3. **Track a Stock:** Personal investments and the stock market play a vital role in a Capitalistic government. Allow students to choose from four different stocks that you will also be following. For two weeks, have students use the newspaper and the Internet to track their stock. They will be responsible for reporting to you whether or not their stock went up or down. Again, you can work with the Math department to help students graph their results. At the end of the project, instruct students to write a short paragraph about what they learned from the experience.

NAME: _____

Crossword Puzzle!

Word List

collapse
decade
distant
enterprise
fragmented
initially
interact

manual
merchant
monopoly
permitted
significant
stock
supply
transport

Across

1. Major
3. To move from one place to another
4. An industry controlled by one person or group
6. A period of ten years
7. Worked or created by hand
10. Mix with
12. Shares of a company
13. Far away

Down

1. The amount available
2. Broken into pieces
5. Allowed
8. At first
9. Someone who sells items at a profit
11. Fall apart
14. A business organization

NAME: _____

 After You Read 📖

Word Search

Find all of the words in the Word Search. Words may be horizontal, vertical, or diagonal. A few may even be backwards! Look carefully!

globalize	nations	collapse	enterprise	supply
decade	strict	consumer	monopoly	exposed
stock	intervention	method	distant	dissolve
transport	merchant	constantly	permitted	operate
manual	demand	bankrupt	corrupt	option
goods	fragmented	foundation	regulate	exception

e	t	g	i	s	t	o	c	k	r	e	h	d	i	k	d	a	t
n	o	h	l	r	w	a	d	i	s	t	a	n	t	g	r	k	f
t	a	p	q	o	n	m	e	t	h	o	d	m	j	d	e	x	r
e	o	e	t	a	b	d	y	y	l	o	p	o	n	o	m	l	a
r	t	r	o	i	l	a	d	e	y	e	h	u	k	f	u	n	g
p	g	m	t	l	o	d	l	t	i	d	t	o	g	k	s	d	m
r	d	i	g	e	y	n	x	i	m	a	n	u	a	l	n	w	e
i	m	t	n	e	s	e	d	l	z	c	h	o	e	r	o	o	n
s	y	t	s	x	w	e	q	a	i	e	s	t	r	i	c	t	t
e	l	e	v	c	a	x	e	f	y	d	l	o	r	j	g	n	e
h	t	d	r	e	o	p	q	o	d	w	f	k	a	g	i	a	d
e	n	p	e	p	u	o	u	u	s	a	e	p	n	o	l	h	k
u	a	i	g	t	l	s	e	n	i	s	s	e	s	r	e	c	c
g	t	k	u	i	y	e	r	d	p	v	a	d	p	t	s	r	o
s	s	i	l	o	l	d	g	a	y	t	n	h	o	e	p	e	r
f	n	f	a	n	p	a	j	t	u	f	f	a	r	f	a	m	r
s	o	h	t	d	p	s	k	i	d	j	e	k	t	w	l	h	u
a	c	r	e	r	u	w	l	o	o	e	q	j	l	i	l	o	p
g	k	t	w	t	s	p	t	n	j	u	m	y	m	w	o	f	t
o	p	e	r	a	t	e	y	g	t	d	t	a	d	v	c	n	h
o	l	e	t	p	u	r	k	n	a	b	g	r	n	u	b	n	s
d	i	s	s	o	l	v	e	e	f	h	b	t	g	d	y	d	o
s	m	d	e	q	r	i	n	t	e	r	v	e	n	t	i	o	n

After You Read

NAME: _____

Comprehension Quiz

Part A

Circle the word **TRUE** if the statement is TRUE **or** Circle the word **FALSE** if it is FALSE.

a) More people moved to cities during the Industrial Revolution.

TRUE   FALSE

b) People are encouraged to open their own businesses in Communist countries.

TRUE   FALSE

c) Small businesses do not benefit from Globalization.

TRUE   FALSE

d) The Russian Revolution led to the fall of Communism in the Soviet Union.

TRUE   FALSE

e) People are free to purchase what they want in a Capitalist country.

TRUE   FALSE

Part B

Match the term on the left with the correct definition on the right.

1	economy		Countries	A
2	consumer		Slowly, over time	B
3	nations		A person that buys goods	C
4	corporations		The management of money	D
5	gradual		Large businesses	E

SUBTOTAL: /10

     World Politics – Big Book CC5777

Part C

Answer the questions in complete sentences.

1. Why did people move from the country to the city during the Industrial Revolution?

③

_____

_____

2. How did President Franklin Delano Roosevelt help the United States recover from the Great Depression?

③

_____

_____

3. How do large businesses benefit from Globalization?

③

_____

_____

4. What impact has technology had on modern business?

③

_____

_____

5. Why does the government protect people from the development of monopolies?

③

_____

_____

SUBTOTAL: /15

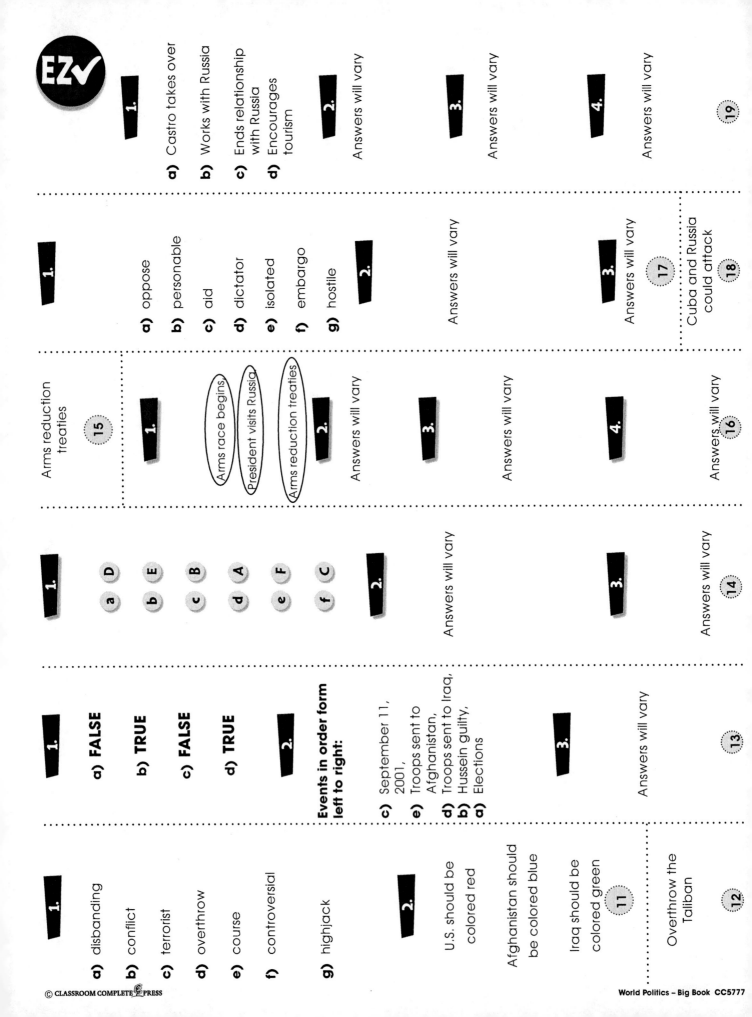

EZ✓

1.
a) Castro takes over
b) Works with Russia
c) Ends relationship with Russia
d) Encourages tourism

2. Answers will vary

3. Answers will vary

4. Answers will vary

19

1.
a) oppose
b) personable
c) aid
d) dictator
e) isolated
f) embargo
g) hostile

2. Answers will vary

3. Answers will vary

17

Cuba and Russia could attack

18

Arms reduction treaties

15

1.
Arms race begins
President visits Russia
Arms reduction treaties

2. Answers will vary

3. Answers will vary

4. Answers will vary

Answers will vary

16

1.
a) D
b) E
c) B
d) A
e) F
f) C

2. Answers will vary

3. Answers will vary

14

1.
a) FALSE
b) TRUE
c) FALSE
d) TRUE

2. Events in order form left to right:
c) September 11, 2001,
e) Troops sent to Afghanistan,
d) Troops sent to Iraq,
b) Hussein guilty,
a) Elections

3. Answers will vary

13

1.
a) disbanding
b) conflict
c) terrorist
d) overthrow
e) course
f) controversial
g) highjack

2.
U.S. should be colored red

Afghanistan should be colored blue

Iraq should be colored green

11

Overthrow the Taliban

12

© CLASSROOM COMPLETE PRESS

World Politics – Big Book CC5777

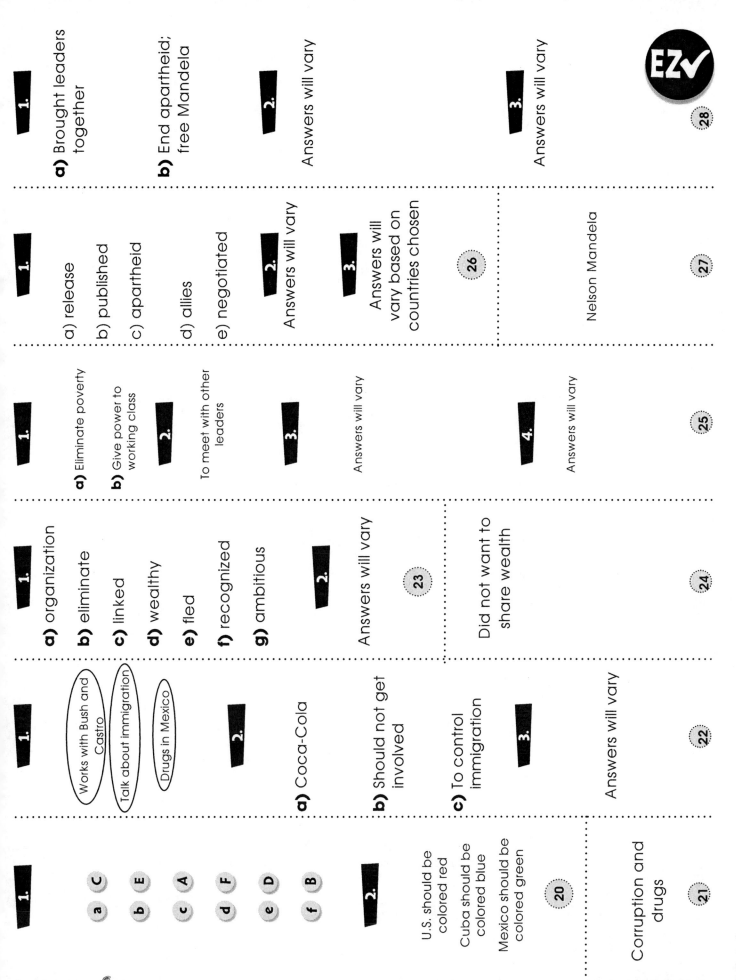

1.
a) Brought leaders together
b) End apartheid; free Mandela

2. Answers will vary

3. Answers will vary

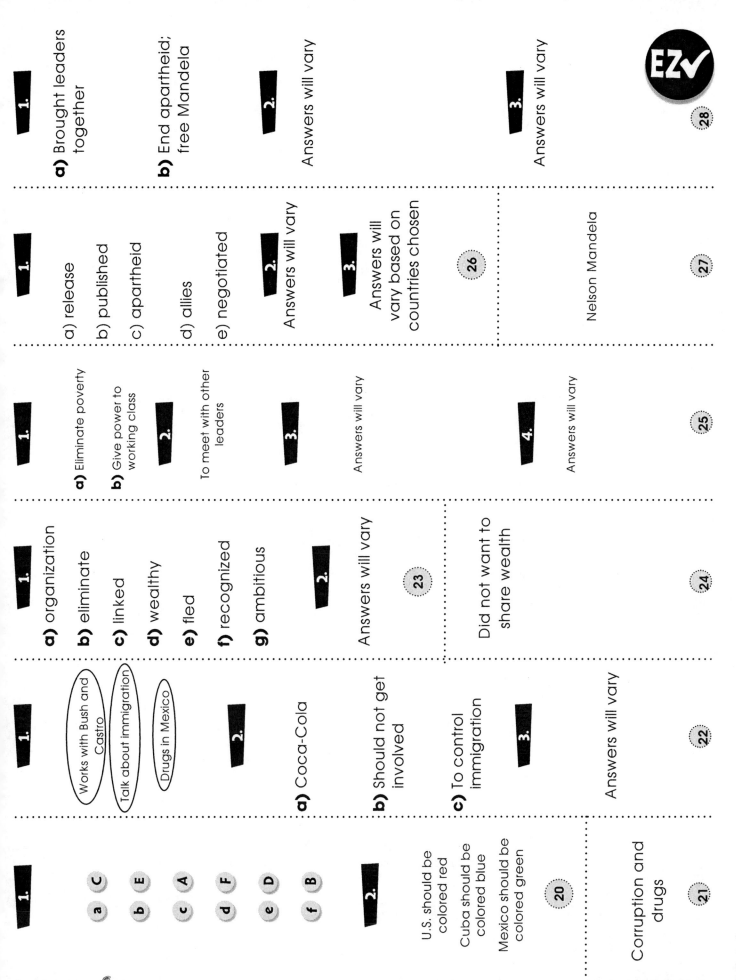
EZ ✓

28

1.
a) release
b) published
c) apartheid
d) allies
e) negotiated

2. Answers will vary

3. Answers will vary based on countries chosen

26

Nelson Mandela

27

1.
a) Eliminate poverty
b) Give power to working class

2. To meet with other leaders

3. Answers will vary

4. Answers will vary

25

1.
a) organization
b) eliminate
c) linked
d) wealthy
e) fled
f) recognized
g) ambitious

2. Answers will vary

23

Did not want to share wealth

24

1.
- Works with Bush and Castro
- Talk about immigration
- Drugs in Mexico

2.
a) Coca-Cola
b) Should not get involved
c) To control immigration

3. Answers will vary

22

1.
a — C
b — E
c — A
d — F
e — D
f — B

2.
U.S. should be colored red
Cuba should be colored blue
Mexico should be colored green

20

Corruption and drugs

21

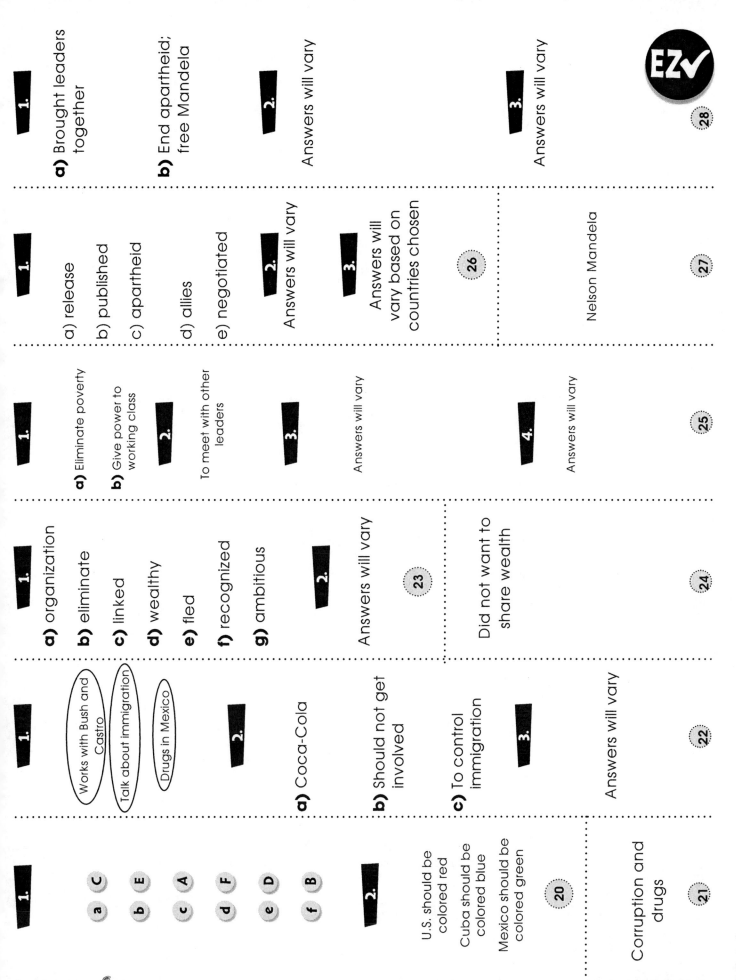

1.

a) Created food surplus
b) Sold surplus for money

2.
Answers will vary

3.
Answers will vary

(37)

1.

a) export
b) assassinate
c) threat
d) surplus
e) fraud

2.
Answers will vary

3.
Answers will vary

(35)

Thought China and Pakistan were threats

(36)

1.

Event in order from left to right:
Not guilty of treason,
Serves 27 years,
World pressures South Africa,
11th President,
Works to stop AIDS epidemic

2.
Answers will vary

3.
Answers will vary

(34)

1.

a) C
b) E
c) B
d) A
e) D

2.
Answers will vary

3.
Answers will vary

(32)

Treason

(33)

1.

a) FALSE
b) TRUE
c) FALSE
d) TRUE
e) TRUE

2.
Answers will vary

3.
Answers will vary

(31)

1.

a) goods
b) coup
c) shortage
d) collapsed
e) citizens

2.
Answers will vary

3.

U.S.
United Kingdom
Cuba

(29)

Let people own businesses

(30)

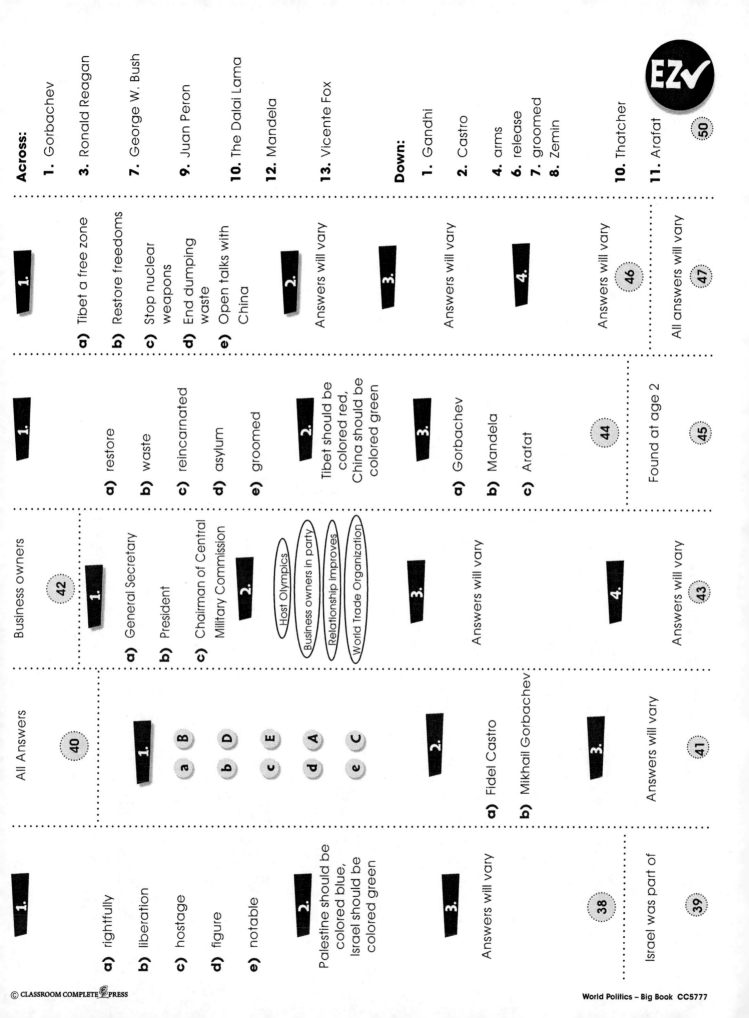

Across:

1. Gorbachev
3. Ronald Reagan
7. George W. Bush
9. Juan Peron
10. The Dalai Lama
12. Mandela
13. Vicente Fox

Down:

1. Gandhi
2. Castro
4. arms
6. release
7. groomed
8. Zemin
10. Thatcher
11. Arafat

1.
a) Tibet a free zone
b) Restore freedoms
c) Stop nuclear weapons
d) End dumping waste
e) Open talks with China

2. Answers will vary

3. Answers will vary

4. Answers will vary

46. Answers will vary

47. All answers will vary

1.
a) restore
b) waste
c) reincarnated
d) asylum
e) groomed

2. Tibet should be colored red, China should be colored green

3.
a) Gorbachev
b) Mandela
c) Arafat

44. Found at age 2

45.

Business owners

42.

1.
a) General Secretary
b) President
c) Chairman of Central Military Commission

2. Host Olympics / Business owners in party / Relationship improves / World Trade Organization

3. Answers will vary

4.

43. Answers will vary

All Answers

40.

1.
a – B
b – D
c – E
d – A
e – C

2.
a) Fidel Castro
b) Mikhail Gorbachev

3. Answers will vary

41.

1.
a) rightfully
b) liberation
c) hostage
d) figure
e) notable

2. Palestine should be colored blue, Israel should be colored green

3. Answers will vary

38. Israel was part of

39.

Word Search Answers

t	e	r	t	f	u	i	s	o	l	a	t	e	d	i	y	d	a
e	e	b	k	c	o	n	f	l	i	c	t	w	i	h	t	k	p
r	u	r	a	r	g	y	v	d	m	g	c	k	a	n	i	c	a
m	y	t	r	e	a	s	o	n	g	j	b	e	a	l	k	a	r
r	g	n	h	o	s	f	d	e	c	a	d	e	w	t	t	j	t
l	o	a	w	s	r	h	o	w	t	m	h	a	d	h	p	h	h
i	t	l	a	e	g	i	t	e	g	o	y	j	f	d	u	g	e
d	k	l	d	g	j	s	s	n	s	u	m	m	i	t	r	i	i
e	r	i	f	e	u	v	c	t	w	f	t	j	d	l	r	h	d
l	k	e	h	l	q	e	a	d	c	o	u	r	s	e	o	t	i
f	c	s	p	d	w	g	z	x	t	u	s	c	h	p	c	w	e
a	f	r	x	m	e	x	p	o	r	t	h	q	e	i	l	d	t
c	u	r	e	c	o	n	o	m	y	h	u	e	t	q	e	i	k
s	c	r	o	w	t	o	j	d	r	y	c	i	g	k	w	r	e
t	h	r	e	a	t	e	a	e	y	u	z	p	n	l	o	h	e
w	d	u	g	l	s	r	s	h	g	e	p	i	d	e	m	i	c
a	o	j	i	a	d	g	u	k	n	v	l	n	r	m	y	e	l
l	y	g	e	e	a	d	u	s	c	z	f	i	m	o	n	f	k
s	k	l	s	w	e	a	l	t	h	y	u	i	s	s	r	h	s
n	e	r	y	e	g	k	y	f	a	d	i	k	j	d	e	e	e
r	r	l	i	b	e	r	a	t	i	o	n	a	r	g	o	y	s
i	f	y	r	t	p	e	r	s	o	n	a	b	l	e	u	o	i
r	e	i	n	c	a	r	n	a	t	e	d	k	f	g	y	e	g

51

Part A

a) FALSE

b) FALSE

c) TRUE

d) FALSE

e) FALSE

Part B

1 **D**

2 **E**

3 **A**

4 **B**

5 **C**

52

EZ✓

Part C

1. Faced problem; Examples will vary

2. Active in politics: Examples will vary

3. Examples will vary

4. Terrorist or peacemaker; Examples will vary

5. Wanted to free Tibet; Examples will vary

53

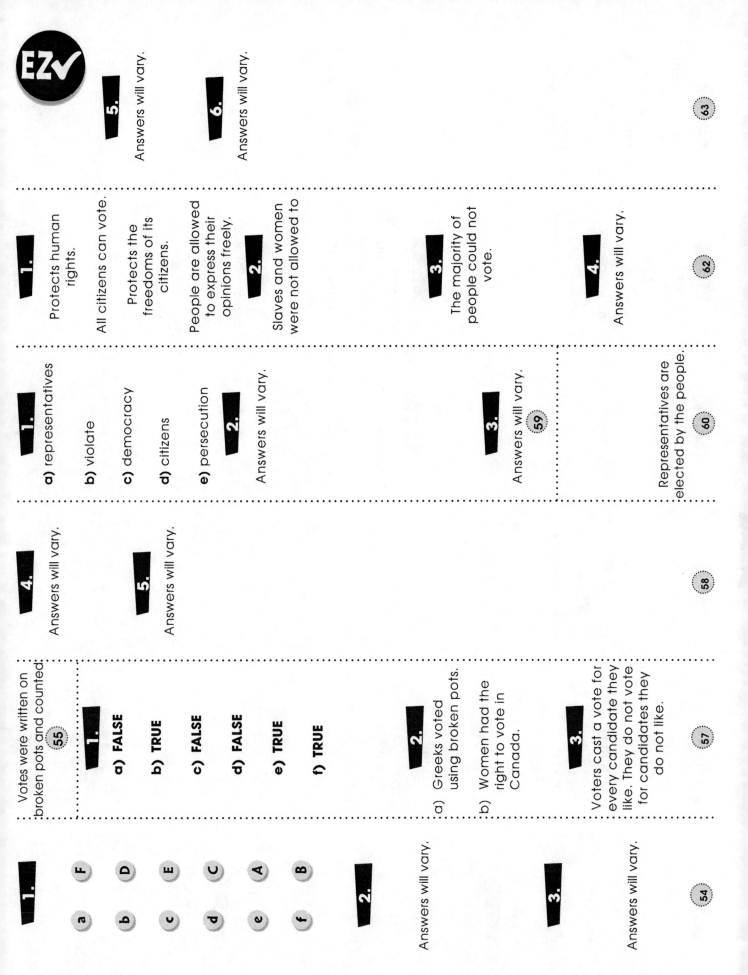

EZ✓

5. Answers will vary.

6. Answers will vary.

(63)

1.
- Protects human rights.
- All citizens can vote.
- Protects the freedoms of its citizens.
- People are allowed to express their opinions freely.

2. Slaves and women were not allowed to vote.

3. The majority of people could not vote.

4. Answers will vary.

(62)

1.
a) representatives
b) violate
c) democracy
d) citizens
e) persecution

2. Answers will vary.

3. Answers will vary. (59)

Representatives are elected by the people. (60)

---

4. Answers will vary.

5. Answers will vary.

(58)

Votes were written on broken pots and counted. (55)

1.
a) FALSE
b) TRUE
c) FALSE
d) FALSE
e) TRUE
f) TRUE

2.
a) Greeks voted using broken pots.
b) Women had the right to vote in Canada.

3. Voters cast a vote for every candidate they like. They do not vote for candidates they do not like.

(57)

1.
F — a
D — b
E — c
C — d
A — e
B — f

2. Answers will vary.

3. Answers will vary.

(54)

4. Parliament selects the prime minister they want. In the presidential system, the people elect their leader. The president may not agree with the other representatives.

5. Answers will vary.

73

1. The head of state approves the prime minister.

Parliament is elected by the people.

Parliament chooses the prime minister.

2. The head of state attends ceremonies and agrees to the laws created by the representatives.

3. Parliament selects a candidate for prime minister. The monarch approves the candidate, who then becomes the prime minister.

72

1.
a) indefinite
b) parliament
c) execute
d) select
e) monarch

2. Answers will vary

69

The three names are prime minister, premier, and president.

70

5. Answers will vary.

6. Answers will vary.

68

A president will veto a bill if he/she does not agree with the bill.

65

1. The president is the head of state and the head of government.

2. Attends ceremonial duties for the president

Is next in line should the president die

Advises the president

3. The president of Puerto Rico can

4. Answers will vary.

67

1.
a) legislature
b) veto
c) bill
d) cabinet
e) term

2. Answers will vary.

3. Answers will vary.

64

EZ✓

5. Answers will vary.

6. Answers will vary.

83

1.
a) FALSE
b) TRUE
c) TRUE
d) FALSE
e) FALSE

2. The minimum age to

3. Voters that do not have confidence in their leader or government do not vote.

4. People register to vote each year on their tax forms. There have been some mistakes, so a few people could not vote.

82

1.
a) eligible
b) enforce
c) suffrage
d) denied
e) fluctuating
f) compulsory

2.

3.

79

People can be fined, made to do community service, or put in jail.

81

5. Answers will vary.

6. Answers will vary.

78

1. There were a large number of dictatorships after World War II. Many dictators were former military leaders. The dictator chooses the people who serve the government.

2. The Roman dictator brought order back during times of trouble.

3. Dictators usually come into power after a war or conflict. The dictators were military leaders in that war or conflict.

4. Roman dictators had rules to follow. Over time, the dictators have taken absolute power.

77

1.
D — a
C — b
E — c
A — d
B — e

2. Answers will vary.

3. Answers will vary.

74

They install a dictator so that one small group has all the power.

75

Crossword Puzzle!

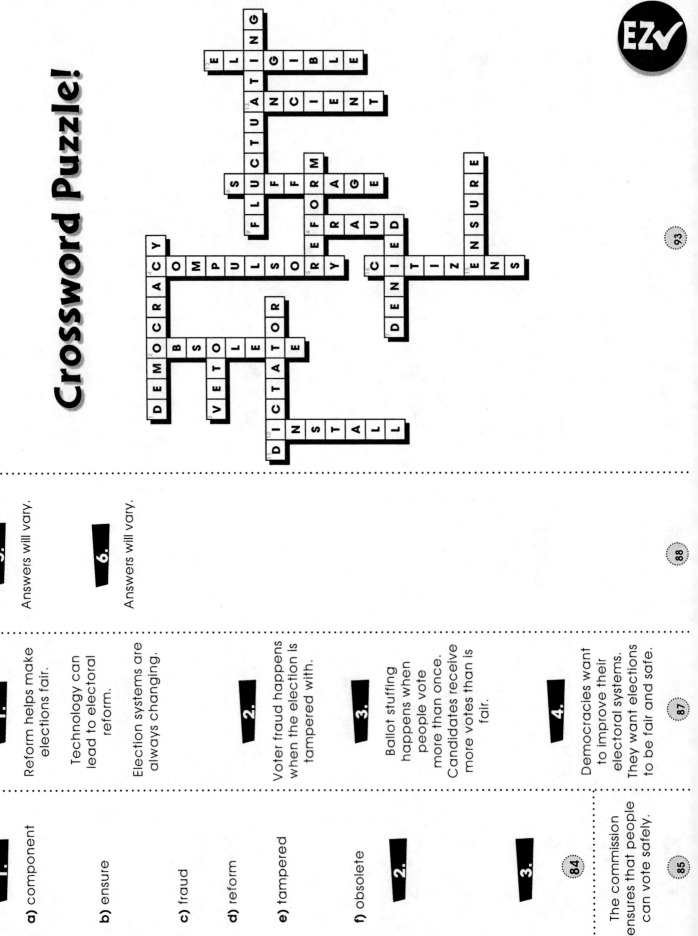

1.

Reform helps make elections fair.

Technology can lead to electoral reform.

Election systems are always changing.

2.

Voter fraud happens when the election is tampered with.

3.

Ballot stuffing happens when people vote more than once. Candidates receive more votes than is fair.

4.

Democracies want to improve their electoral systems. They want elections to be fair and safe.

1.

a) component

b) ensure

c) fraud

d) reform

e) tampered

f) obsolete

2.

3.

The commission ensures that people can vote safely.

5.

Answers will vary.

6.

Answers will vary.

Word Search Answers

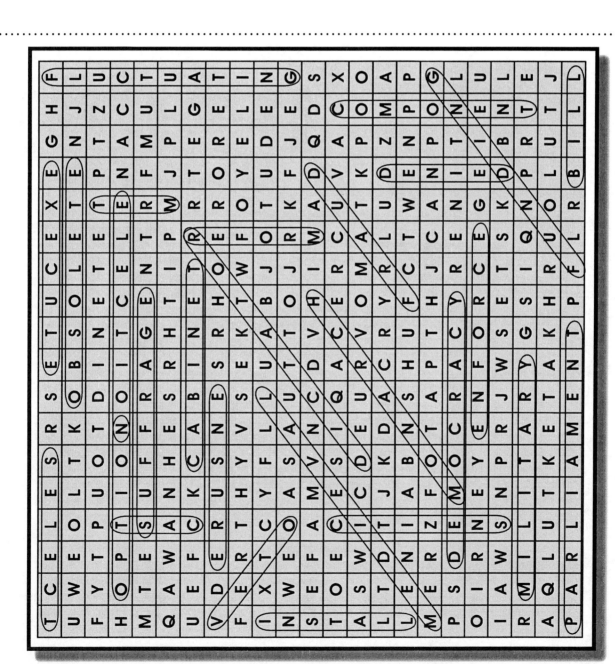

Part A

a) FALSE

b) TRUE

c) FALSE

d) FALSE

e) TRUE

Part B

1 C

2 A

3 D

4 E

5 B

95

Part C

1. The cabinet advises the leader.

2. Technology can make elections easier, faster, and more fair.

3. A prime minister's term lasts as long as they have Parliament's support.

4. Race, religion, gender, social status, and age are all reasons people have been denied the right to vote.

5. Voter turnout is higher in countries with compulsory voting.

96

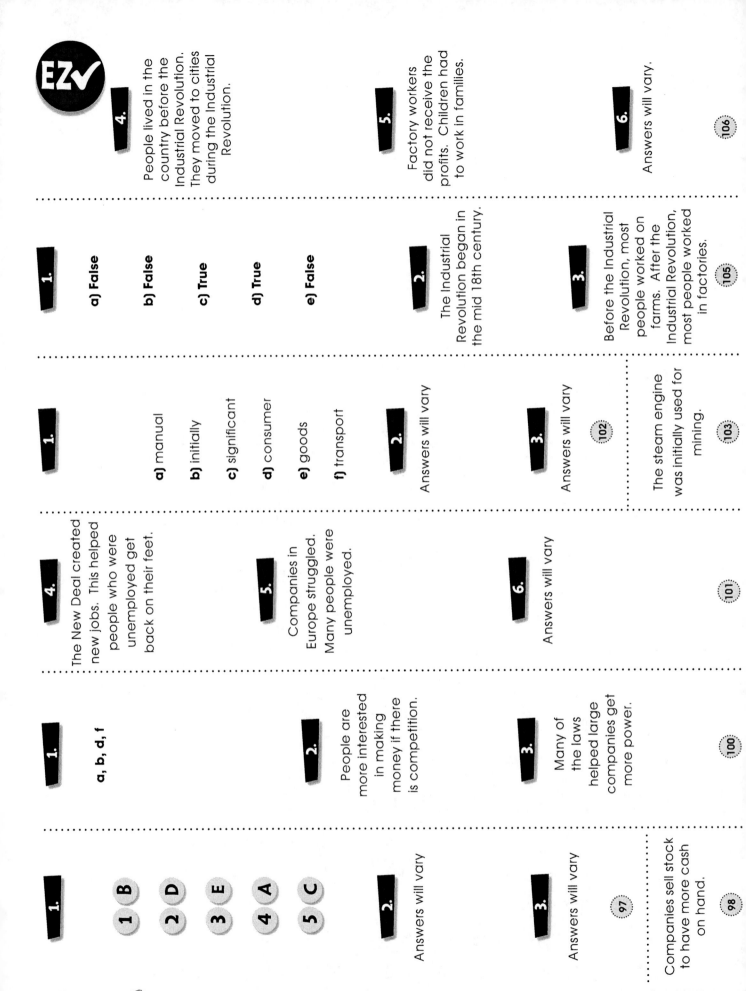

EZ✓

4. People lived in the country before the Industrial Revolution. They moved to cities during the Industrial Revolution.

5. Factory workers did not receive the profits. Children had to work in families.

6. Answers will vary.

(106)

1.
a) False
b) False
c) True
d) True
e) False

2. The Industrial Revolution began in the mid 18th century.

3. Before the Industrial Revolution, most people worked on farms. After the Industrial Revolution, most people worked in factories.

(105)

1.
a) manual
b) initially
c) significant
d) consumer
e) goods
f) transport

2. Answers will vary

3. Answers will vary

(102)

The steam engine was initially used for mining.

(103)

4. The New Deal created new jobs. This helped people who were unemployed get back on their feet.

5. Companies in Europe struggled. Many people were unemployed.

6. Answers will vary

(101)

1.
a, b, d, f

2. People are more interested in making money if there is competition.

3. Many of the laws helped large companies get more power.

(100)

1.
1 B
2 D
3 E
4 A
5 C

2. Answers will vary

3. Answers will vary

(97)

Companies sell stock to have more cash on hand.

(98)

1.

a) dissolve

b) conflict

c) exception

d) method

2.

Answers will vary

107

Capitalist countries and Communist countries disagreed.

108

1.

Communism- Eastern Europe, Cuba, the Soviet Union

Capitalism- The United States, the United Kingdom, Western Europe

2.

Both wanted more power in the world.

3.

The Soviet Union changed from a Communist to a Capitalist economy. The country was divided into several smaller countries.

4.

Answers will vary

109

1.

a) option

b) demand

c) foundation

d) regulate

e) supply

2.

Answers will vary

3.

Answers will vary

110

Prices are determined by the law of supply and demand.

111

1.

a) False

b) True

c) True

d) False

2.

Prices rise when there is a high demand. Prices go down when there is a low demand.

3.

Answers will vary

112

4.

Answers will vary

5.

Answers will vary

113

1.

1 C

2 D

3 A

4 E

5 B

2.

Answers will vary

3.

Answers will vary

114

Capitalism became an important political economy during the Industrial Revolution.

116

1.

a, b & e

2.

People can own their own businesses and sell whatever they want.

3.

More people started owning their own businesses.

4.

Monopolies lead to corruption. Prices go up.

5.

Answers will vary

117

EZ✓

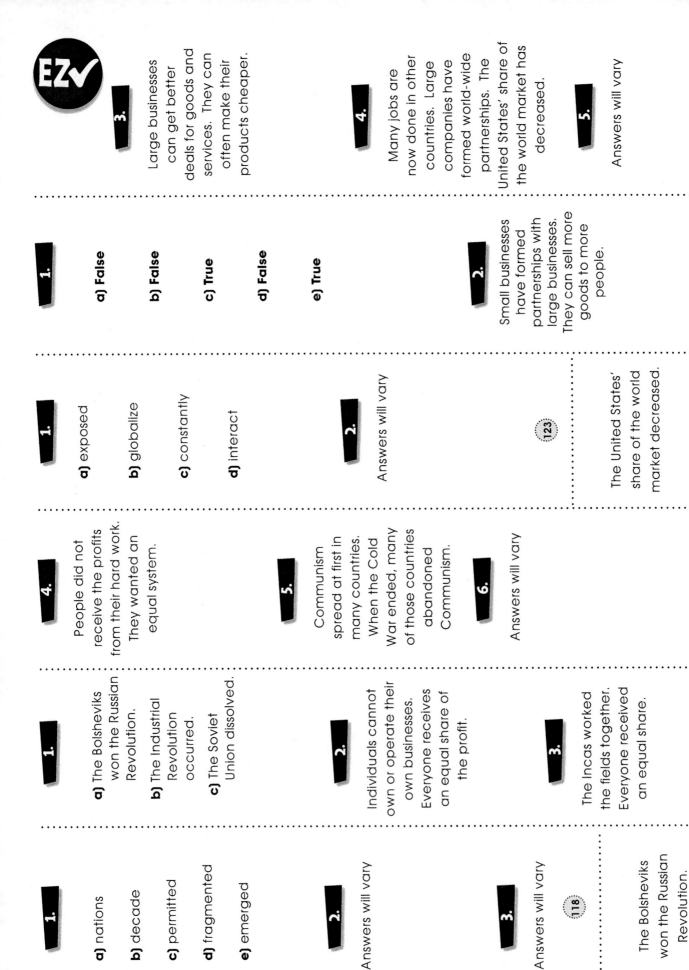

EZ✓

3.
Large businesses can get better deals for goods and services. They can often make their products cheaper.

4.
Many jobs are now done in other countries. Large companies have formed world-wide partnerships. The United States' share of the world market has decreased.

5.
Answers will vary

1.
a) False
b) False
c) True
d) False
e) True

2.
Small businesses have formed partnerships with large businesses. They can sell more goods to more people.

1.
a) exposed
b) globalize
c) constantly
d) interact

2.
Answers will vary

The United States' share of the world market decreased.

4.
People did not receive the profits from their hard work. They wanted an equal system.

5.
Communism spread at first in many countries. When the Cold War ended, many of those countries abandoned Communism.

6.
Answers will vary

1.
a) The Bolsheviks won the Russian Revolution.
b) The Industrial Revolution occurred.
c) The Soviet Union dissolved.

2.
Individuals cannot own or operate their own businesses. Everyone receives an equal share of the profit.

3.
The Incas worked the fields together. Everyone received an equal share.

1.
a) nations
b) decade
c) permitted
d) fragmented
e) emerged

2.
Answers will vary

3.
Answers will vary

The Bolsheviks won the Russian Revolution.

1.

a) gradual

b) distant

c) collapse

d) strict

2.

Answers will vary

Life is too difficult in Cuba because of the trade situation.

3.

Answers will vary

1.

China

Cuba

Vietnam

North Korea

Laos

2.

People can now own their own businesses.

3.

U.S. citizens cannot visit Cuba. The United States will not trade with Cuba.

4.

Answers will vary

5.

Answers will vary

Across:

1. significant

3. transport

4. monopoly

6. decade

7. manual

10. interact

12. stock

13. distant

Down:

1. supply

2. fragmented

5. permitted

8. initially

9. merchant

11. collapse

14. enterprise

Part C

1. People began working in large factories in the city.

2. He supported the New Deal which created new jobs.

3. Large businesses can get cheaper prices on goods and workers.

4. People can now do business with anyone in the world.

5. Monopolies can raise prices unfairly.

Part A

a) True

b) False

c) False

d) False

e) True

Part B

1. D

2. C

3. A

4. E

5. B

Word Search Answers

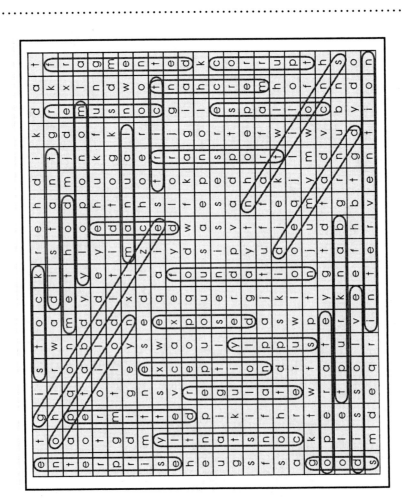

Effect

Reagan, Thatcher, and Gorbachev work to
end Cold War

Effect

Reagan, Thatcher, and Gorbachev work to
end Cold War